CW00675051

OFF THE CLUFF

Praise for Algy Cluff's
previous books

Get On With It

'At seventy-six, he reflects in this memoir on a blissful sounding life at home and abroad – high jinks in the Army, languorous City luncheons primed by pink gins, drilling successfully for oil in the North Sea, mining diamonds in Africa and becoming friendly with such disparate figures as Margaret Thatcher and Zimbabwe's notorious President Robert Mugabe...

Enjoyably gossipy, *Get On With It* also contains valuable insights into business and political life... Appropriately, playwright Sir Tom Stoppard suggests his next book should be called *The Importance Of Being Algy*.'

—*Daily Mail*

'... one of the few books I'd read which I wished longer...'

—Charles Moore, *The Spectator*

'When he was a small boy at boarding school in the 1940s, Algy Cluff's imagination was captivated by hectic tales of derring-do in the novels of John Buchan. He resolved then to actualise this imaginary world of Clubland heroes. For the past half-century he has been, as this rattling, full-throttled, red-blooded memoir shows, a strenuous, venturesome capitalist in Richard Hannay's mould.'

—Richard Davenport-Hines, *TLS*

'A cross-pollination of James Bond and Indiana Jones, with an eye for adventure and a real talent for entrepreneurship.'

—*KCW Today*

Unsung Heroes

'… a splendid book…'

—*The Times*

'I warmly recommend it… Although Algy's own life has been extremely active and successful, his greatest gift is for describing, affectionately, lives of which this could not be said.'

—Charles Moore, *The Spectator*

Off the Cluff

Algy Cluff

Cluff & Sons

First published in Great Britain in 2021 by Cluff & Sons

Copyright © J.G. Cluff 2021

J.G. Cluff has asserted his right under the Copyright, Designs and Patents Act 1988 to be identified as the author of this work.

F. E. Smith image courtesy of John Springs.

Extracts from *Journey to Java* by kind permission of Adam Nicolson.

Every reasonable effort has been made to trace copyright holders of material reproduced in this book, but if any have been inadvertently overlooked the publishers would be glad to hear from them.

Edited, designed and produced by Tandem Publishing
http://tandempublishing.yolasite.com

ISBN: 978-1-9168994-0-7

10 9 8 7 6 5 4 3 2 1

A CIP catalogue record for this book is available from the British Library.

Dedicated to Ronald Winston and Paul Irby.
Two friends of over fifty years' standing.

And in memory of Nicholas Berry
(1942–2016).

And of Andrea von Stumm.

Also by Algy Cluff:

Get on With It

Unsung Heroes

By The Way

Contents

FOREWORD

Taki Theodoracopulos

HERE AT LAST is my chance to get a word in before Algy. For any of you who know Algy Cluff, this is obviously a joke. Never have I met a man of fewer words and more accomplishments. Writers who are also raconteurs generally spill the beans at the dinner table and leave the readers holding the can. Not so Algy. He is as measured with his words as a Taiwanese spy deeply embedded in the Pyongyang Ministry of Defence.

And yet he is a great teller of tales. Algy's writing has one of the rare qualities: an original voice that is his own; which is to say, it is *sotto voce*, discreet, very English, and very funny. Such spontaneity is not the easiest note for a writer to reach but the hardest. Algy believes in private enterprise, prefers being rich to being poor, strong rather than weak, clean rather than dirty, free rather than socialist. This stuff will get him nowhere in the literary world, as one can well imagine. He is a conundrum, coming from a privileged background but starting from scratch. He cannot even claim hunger and cold to have motivated him. Instead, he writes about people without a hint of negativity or hate, surely something modern-age amateur shrinks would classify as mental anaemia.

This is Algy's fourth tome of memoirs, all four gratefully short and to the point. Is there anyone that Algy hasn't met, shot with, partied with, crossed swords or done business with? Is there any club in the whole wide world that Algy does not belong as a member? On the evidence before me, the answer is a resounding no. I got to know Algy well during the two weeks we sat next to each other in Court 13 on the Strand during a libel case a merry widow, now long dead, had brought against *The Spectator* after an article I had written. Algy remained impassive throughout, while I wanted to throw an inkwell at the judge.

After serving his country as a Grenadier Guard officer and having seen action in Borneo and Cyprus, Algy turned to the oil business, opening up markets the world over, especially with North Sea oil. Any other Brit with his record, especially with his charities, would have been by now a long-time member of the Upper House, but Algy suffers from a rare condition that makes it impossible for him to toady to greasy politicians, hence his OBE rather than ermine.

And his wonderful and very comely wife Blondel gets a whole chapter in his latest opus, one headed as BWM, no, not what you think, but black wives matter. I know and love Blondel, and have also met one of his three boys, Harry, and he's a delight. One thing about Algy that gets mentioned here and there, but never in any detail, is the fact that he belongs to more clubs than any other living person in the whole wide world. I once ran into Algy on St James's, and a bit under the weather I asked him if there was a club on any side of that famous street that he didn't belong to. He pointed to a street just off St James's and Wilton's. 'But Wilton's a restaurant, not a club,' I spluttered. He had made his point. In America it's more of the same: yacht clubs, golf clubs, racquet clubs, gentlemen's clubs, ditto in Africa. It gets so bad, just before writing this foreword I rang up the Kit-Kat Club in downtown Bangui of the Central African Republic. A blackball there means being boiled alive. Yes, you guessed it,

'Monsieur Cluff est une membre du committee.' There were also rumours about an Algius Cluffus corpse among the ashes of a Pompeii club in 79 A.D., but they have never been confirmed.

Dignity, selfless courage, and an ability to make and keep great friends is what makes Algy Cluff tick. Read on and remember how enjoyable life used to be.

OFF THE CLUFF

1

Black Wives Matter

IN September 1993 I married my Caribbean
bride Blondel in St Stephen's Chapel,
Stanley, Hong Kong. She was given away
by Henry Keswick and the Best Man was the
legendary David Tang, to whom in 1980 I had
given his first job. As my bride's parents had
recently split up, the families agreed that we
should undertake a virtual elopement to Asia.
The small congregation comprised my friends
who lived and worked in Hong Kong, in particular Julian and Rexi Reid whose daughter,
Sarah – my goddaughter – acted as a demure
bridesmaid; James Filmer-Wilson, who continues to live and work there; Simon Keswick
and Percy and Clara Weatherall who were there
on Jardine business; Evelyn Cromer, enigmatic
Asian-based businessman; Charles Letts, controversial Singapore-based buccaneer, Don Liu,
quiet and clever banker with his handsome
mother Pearl and two glamorous sisters; Simon

Murray, then outstanding Chief Executive of Hutchison Whampoa; David Lie, entrepreneur and son of a Nationalist General; Jack and Ruth King, friends from Cambridge where Jack was the Bursar of Wolfson College; Mark Birley, King of Clubs, and, rather surprisingly Andrew, the then Duke of Devonshire who was en poste in Hong Kong along with a lady friend. Other than Andrew, Jack King, David Tang and Charles Letts I am able to report that happily all these are alive and well.

The reception was truncated by reason of an approaching typhoon which the Chinese regard as auspicious and which proved to be an omen for our marriage. Blondel and I were whisked away as newlyweds in Tang's Bentley with Alex, his egregious manservant at the wheel and delivered to number 9 Shek O, one of the Jardine 'bungalows' and decidedly my favourite house outside of Britain with its sweeping views across the South China Sea. Our first evening as man and wife was a strange one – as Alex had managed to crash the vintage Bentley after depositing us at the house – depriving Blondel of her trousseau. She and I, therefore, both dined dressed in my golfing gear!

The reason I mention this is not because we were married in Hong Kong, although that certainly is indelibly impressed on my mind, but that as far as I am aware it was the first time someone of my generation actually married a black lady. And I should say at once that at no time have we as a couple experienced any form of prejudice within our circle – quite the reverse in fact. Although shortly afterwards I was asked to lunch by the very grand Chief Executive of one of the world's largest mining companies in Johannesburg. We were standing having a cocktail before lunch, waited on by a white butler. In the distance there were four or five black waiters chatting by a serving hatch. I should explain that one of the more derogatory words in vulgar use there at that time to describe an African was *munt*. My host turned to the butler and said, 'Tell those munts to stop chattering, it's getting on my nerves.'

The butler departed on his errand. 'Hold on,' I said, 'I am married to a "munt", if you don't mind.'

'So you are, a very attractive girl she is too,' he said without a trace of apology, or embarrassment. How some things have improved!

I had met my handsome and statuesque wife through a colleague of hers at Lazard, the merchant bank, where Blondel, being a solicitor, headed the legal department she had created thanks to the opportunity given her by Sir John Nott. By descent she is from Anguilla, an island which for some years she valiantly represented as its diplomat to the UK and EU, based in London. She and her four brothers belong to two prominent local families whose links with the island span centuries. Anguilla, although populated by no more than fifteen thousand souls, has always punched above its weight, producing per capita a very high number of successful sportsmen as well as producing ladies of singular beauty, of which Blondel is certainly one.

I have observed her trajectory from a thirty-year-old solicitor to, thirty years later, the award of the CBE for services to numismatics and to the West Indian Community. The circumstances of the award included some comedy at my expense. I had just been invested with an OBE at Buckingham Palace for, in my case, services to charity and business, and I took my wife and sons to the investiture and to lunch afterwards at the Turf Club. When we returned to our house in Westminster, I spotted a formal and rather familiar envelope on the hall table. This turned out to be a letter to Blondel from the Lord Chancellor offering her the award of the CBE, so within three hours of being awarded the OBE I had been trumped by my wife. 'Congratulations,' I hissed between clenched teeth!

Blondel's industry and commitment are indeed admirable. Apart from resurrecting the West India Committee, where she became CEO, guiding that charity from its sugar-dominated colonial past to a vibrant champion of the Caribbean's history and future, she is variously on the advisory committee of The Royal Mint and is the Chairman of the National Lottery Community Fund. Through her exertions much was done during her tour of duty as Anguilla's representative to the European Union, including the construction of the Cluff Maternity Hospital and the raising of £220 million to deal with the ravages of Hurricane Irma. She has recently been co-opted onto the so-called Windrush Cross-Government Working Group to investigate what can be done in terms of restitution in response to one of Britain's less than sensible Home Office policies, whilst applying the rules of common sense. My in-laws, both now dead, were of the Windrush generation who nobly responded to Churchill's call to come to the aid of the Mother Country after the war leaving behind, in their case, a safe bucolic environment of farming and fishing. It is a very poor reflection on our soi-disant good nature that only in 2020 has an effort been made to resolve this disconcerting occurrence. My wife is therefore in no way resting on her laurels and will continue to champion the cause of the people of the Caribbean, alongside tireless work for England's heritage. Amongst her more important achievements recently has been her realisation of the side-lining of West Indian soldiers during two World Wars which she has sought to correct by the production of two books, along with David Wells, a member of the staff of the West India Committee.

In paying this tribute to my wife I am also able to draw on forty years of African experience and knowledge and respect I have developed for the intelligence and commercial leadership of many African women. They are rightly taking centre stage now and it is hoped that the day will come when African women lead all their countries away from the avarice which has characterised so much of Africa's recent 'leadership'. Black wives do indeed matter and flourish.

I would not characterise life with a black lady as necessarily smooth – there are many differences which need careful consideration. Two examples are hair and music. Hair is of paramount importance in Black Women's lives.

In my wife's case there is so much of the stuff and its cultivation takes considerable effort. It seems to need feeding, takes hours to wash, can be styled in a multitude of ways. 'Up or down?' is a question I am asked every evening. Blondel claims that she married me only because of my impressive Afro (which is in fact, the bearskin I wore whilst on ceremonial duties as a Grenadier!). Her myopia was to be my good fortune.

Music is everywhere and so I have a sound-proof study. Dancing – I am considered to rate 0 out of 10. My dancing, to use another military metaphor, is akin to marching on the spot. I have made many attempts to convey to my wife my skill in this department – none of them successful. Nearly all occurred on the small dance floor at Annabel's, a nightclub founded by my friend Mark Birley in 1963 when I joined it (although I have been disenfranchised by its new owner Richard Caring for the sin of age). I particularly recall an occasion when I took to the dance floor, having advised the disc jockey of my request: 'Love Me Love My Dog'. The rascal wrongfooted me – literally – by playing 'I Will Survive' by Gloria Gaynor. Survive I did not; since then Blondel has come to terms with my dancing, adding peripheral gestures and considerable rhythm whilst I am allowed to focus singularly on my march to freedom.

Singing is another void in my make-up, despite frequent attempts on my part to demonstrate latent talent. On one occasion after lunch at the Royal St George's Golf Club I was driving my wife and sons Harry and Philip back home and was instructed yet again by them to play CD 2 track 6, so this time I sang along in a spirited rendition of 'Drop It Like It's Hot', rapping along with Snoop Dogg as best as I could, which I found quite fulfilling. Was I thanked by my family? *Please never do that again Dad*, I was instructed, with my wife included!

But above all Black mothers matter, and I can ever attest to their loyalty and devotion to the cause of their children, whose interests in every context are paramount, something I applaud in both my wife and my late mother-in-law, Cora.

2

NEW YORK

I LIVED IN New York for six months in 1966, having been appointed by the Ionian Bank as their North American Representative. This resulted in no benefit to the bank but conferred some faux consequence on myself. It was a vivid episode in my life – for the first time liberated from Public School or Army controls. In the six months after my resignation from the Army I had been living off the generosity of my father, following my convincing him to invest heavily (and successfully) in the rubber plantation sector in Malaysia. I continued to draw on these funds when in New York. Initially I stayed at the Yale Club before taking over John Guinness's apartment at 131 East 66th Street. He was U Thant's personal assistant at the UN.

This was the start of a constant love affair with New York which obtains to this day. I really went there because my Grenadier contemporary, Jasper Larken, had gone to work on

Wall Street and I had thought I would spend a couple of weeks there with him. The first day I navigated my way downtown to lunch with Jasper at his office on Wall Street. I emerged from the subway and became rather lost in the network of small streets and vast buildings. I approached a large black lady selling flowers and enquired whether she could direct me to Wall Street. 'You are standing in it you c**t,' came the concise answer. I found this directness rather appealing after the tergiversations of English conversation. Another example occurred when I flagged down a cab, which in those days were all driven by Americans rather than Indians and Africans as is the case now. 'Could you take me to the Racquet Club please?' I asked. 'Waddya mean please' he shot back, presumably judging that address to be rather patronising.

But my real and enduring pleasure derived from life in New York over sixty years has undoubtedly been the people I have known. I already knew an amazing character, Evverts Wren Fulton, whom I have referred to elsewhere as we had been contemporaries at Stowe. Evverts had a high IQ and abundant charm. Alas he stood rather too close to the cocktail cabinet and was run over by a truck as he was leaving a bar in the Lower East Side. After a long period in hospital his family rented an apartment for him together with a carer, as he was now immobile. Jasper and I visited him from time to time. After I had returned to London, Jasper one day could not gain admittance to the apartment and, together with the building's janitor, smashed his way in to find poor Evverts dead on a sofa, the only remaining piece of furniture in the apartment – the carer, it transpired, having sold everything else and disappeared, never to be seen again.

Other enduring friendships that happily still obtain were with Louis Pemberton, Bobby Power (mentioned elsewhere) and George Zahringer III. Pemberton, scion of one of the original founding families, is a Princeton man and gifted with immense charm complemented by a handsome facial cast. I met him in 1966, at which point he lived on the edge of Harlem. We became firm friends and spent much time at the Union Club, 69th and Park, a splendid building endowed with a vast library.

Lou in those days worked at Lehman Brothers on the broking side. He built up a strong clientele in Britain and made frequent trips here, spending weekends with the d'Avigdor-Goldsmid family at Somerhill, an enormous house in Kent. On one visit, musing about his ancient lineage, he concluded that he was related to the Kent Leigh-Pemberton family. At that time Robin Leigh-Pemberton was the Governor of the Bank of England. Lou called the bank and was put straight through to the Governor, who asked him over to lunch, reflecting great credit on the Governor's lack of pomposity. They became firm friends. Lou married a second time very happily to Suzanne, an accomplished artist. He remains an active broker in his nineties and enjoys a fruitful cooperation with a correspondingly competent and discreet London-based stockbroker, Paul Irby, formerly a partner in Vickers, da Costa and Strauss Turnbull. He is also still working, although a few years younger than Lou.

***

In the early 1990s I was staying with my wife at Deepdale Golf Club in Manhasset on Long Island. Membership of this club was and is much sought after. It was decidedly a rich man's club with a handsome Clubhouse, previously a Whitney family house, and a first-class golf course. All that the members had in common was that they were rich; otherwise they were an unusual combination of Jewish, Aristocratic and Cosmopolitan. For many years it had been run with a rod of iron by a partner in the prominent investment bank Allen & Co, Terry Kramer. Kramer became a legend. He was popularly known as a 'Club Buster', being congenitally unable to cope with the idea of being excluded from any of the world's most exclusive clubs. He had married the boss's daughter, a formidable and beautiful lady herself. I enjoyed accelerated membership by way of the recommendation of the remarkable lawyer-cum-businessman Derald Ruttenberg, Kramer's bosom friend, with whom I used to shoot for many years at the Gannochy Estate in Angus.

Although no golfer I had a number of friends who were members. Alexander Marchessini, George McFadden and Bobby Power amongst them. I used to occasionally zigzag around the course, sometimes alone, although there is a rule that even if playing alone one must have a caddie, of whom there were a number of 'characters' – who also became friends. When I was in New York on business I used to prefer to stay at Deepdale as not only is it peaceful, but the Clubhouse was comfortable with excellent service and food. Two Irish brothers called Heaney managed it, and by this time Kramer had joined the great club in the sky and had been succeeded by an equally able President, D. Dixon Boardman, who has now presided over the club with exemplary flair for thirty years. On the evening in question there was unusually another couple staying, who turned out to be George Zahringer III and his wife. We dined together and it transpired that George, then a banker with Deutsche Bank, was a golfer of some considerable consequence – playing I think to +3 at the age of fifty. I played with him a few times, once at the famous National Links, and he was generally on the green having smoked two cigarettes by the time my caddie and I lumbered into view. George, at my instigation, joined the Royal St George's Club in Sandwich, now one of his favourite golfing destinations.

So, in New York over the last sixty years, I have had the privilege of the friendship of Ronald Winston (of whom I have written in a previous book), Bobby Power, Louis Pemberton, George Zahringer III and more recently Hugh Tilney. In 1992 I joined the Brook Club, an outstanding establishment with the finest club food and club staff of anywhere as well as the most charming private dining room. The Brook has a strong Anglo-American bias and, like Deepdale, is ruled with benign firmness by 'Mungo' Meehan, a cocktail of shrewdness, charm and humour who has maintained the highest standards.

For how many more years I shall be spared I dare not hazard, but certainly I hope to maintain the exhilarating New York dimension to my life.

3

THREE CAPTAINS
AND ONE WIFE

I N THE 1960s there served together in the
Royal Horse Guards (the Blues) three
officers who not only shared the same regiment but also the same wife. She was called
Julia Williamson. Possessed of average looks
and intelligence, she nonetheless won these
three officers: Darel de Sausmarez Carey, Sir
Nicholas Nuttall and Lord Patrick Beresford,
the last a man of some consequence. All are
now dead.

The first husband, Captain Darel de
Sausmarez Carey, I knew slightly for some
years. He was handsome and undeniably
charming although wholly unreliable. I had
a strange tangential experience following on
from the failure of his investment advisory
business – Sausmarez Carey & Harris, which
he set up when he left the Army. In 1995 I had
an office at 58 St James's Street. One morning

I received a curious letter from the Major General commanding London District, whom I had never met. Indeed, I had left the Army ten years before and was then enjoying some minor celebrity based on assumptions by the press that my interests in the North Sea's Buchan Oil Field were worth many millions. To my astonishment, not to mention my bank manager's, that year I materialised on the *Sunday Times* Rich List at number 201, when in reality I had no money at all! The Major General's letter intriguingly invited me to lunch with him at The Ritz hotel so that he could discuss a matter, as he put it, of 'National Importance'. What on earth could this be?

I had to wait a week, when there I was sitting at a table for two with the General by one of those famous pillars in that ornate room. We ate our way through three courses chatting about this and that. Finally, the coffee materialised and with it the matter of National Importance. 'Can you lend me £100,000,' he said, going rather pink. It transpired that my new friend had fallen for the blandishments of Captain Carey and had guaranteed his overdraft, which had been called in following the failure of Sausmarez Carey & Harris.

'I am sorry,' I replied, 'but all my money is

still 500 metres below the North Sea.'

'But I thought you were the 201st richest man in Britain,' he said indignantly. We never met again.

Husband number two was Patrick Beresford, to whom I shall return. Husband number three was an amiable Baronet of Yorkshire/Cheshire heritage whose fortune was derived from Edmund Nuttall, Sons and Co, road builders. His father, Sir Keith, died on active service in 1941 with the Royal Engineers. Nicholas, sandy haired and very much the Yorkshireman in appearance, went from Eton via Sandhurst to the Blues, being commissioned in 1953. His marriage to Julia lasted four years only. He remained in the Army until 1968 when he left to chair the family business. Like so many of his generation he went into tax exile in the Bahamas where he sensibly married his fourth wife, a local girl, Eugenie McWeeney, by whom he had a son to add to his heir Harry and four daughters.

I return to Patrick Beresford, Julia's second marriage into the Blues. I would judge him to be one of the most competent and admirable men of our generation but his choice of wife was to terminate his chosen military career, which otherwise I am confident would have led to the highest military rank. Patrick was the younger brother of the Marquess of Waterford, who inherited the magnificent Curraghmore Estate in County Waterford. I met Patrick when he, as a Captain in the Blues, and I, a Captain in the Grenadiers, joined the Guards Independent Parachute Company in 1963. That company was the pathfinder for the UK's so-called Strategic Reserves at that time. Patrick was the Intelligence Officer and we did two tours overseas – in Cyprus in 1963 and Borneo in 1964.

In Borneo we became attached to the SAS and were known during that period of duty as the Guards Squadron, SAS. I had mixed feelings about this plan, not being one of nature's voluntary heroes, but Patrick flourished. I spent all our Borneo time in the jungle on patrol with three other guardsmen, whilst Patrick remained on the coast at a Chinese river town, Sibu, in Sarawak. We communicated by Morse code and one evening I was advised that Patrick was coming by helicopter to join us for two weeks as aerial photographs had revealed that just across the border from Sarawak in Indonesian Borneo's Kalimantan there was a stockade thought to house an Indonesian army detachment, whom it was our duty to deny entry into Sarawak by summoning up Gurkha reinforcements. To my consternation, Patrick advised me that he would accompany me to the border – a ridge of mountains – and from there I should proceed into Kalimantan together with six Punan braves.

These Punans were hunter-gatherers who ranged throughout the jungle regions of Sarawak. They were primitive folk whose diet was primarily Sago with an occasional monkey, which they killed with darts tipped with strychnine and fired through a five-foot-long blowpipe. I have written of them elsewhere, but in an amusing and rather embarrassing inversion of the rule that the intrepid white man discovers a primitive tribe, in our case they discovered us blundering through the jungle. Reminiscent of a *Punch* cartoon in the 1950s depicting two white men in solar topees arriving at what looks like the Victoria Falls, being greeted by tribesmen whose leader says: 'Yes they are splendid Falls aren't they – thank you for coming along and discovering them for us!'

At any rate (one of Patrick Beresford's standard expressions) there I found myself after three days trekking on top of the ridge and about to invade Indonesia illegally. I had not the foggiest idea how I was going to find the stockade and would be totally reliant on my Punan friends to achieve that objective. To my relief I had strict instructions on no account to engage with the enemy, which instructions accurately reflected my own intentions. My task, therefore, guided by the Punans, was to find the stockade and determine whether it was manned by the Indonesian army or was in fact deserted. Eventually, after another three days of clambering down the other side of the ridge, we came upon a river and there on the other side on a bend in the river was our objective. For two hours we rested and watched for any sign of life, of which thankfully there was none! However, it was obvious that it had recently been occupied so we had to manoeuvre ourselves – or swim – across the river. I was incapable of swimming whilst simultaneously holding a loaded rifle, so one of my Punan friends volunteered to convey my rifle across the river. We duly searched the stockade and collected notebooks and other ephemera before beginning our return to the ridge and the relative safety of Sarawak. Patrick had remained alone for what must have been three rather nerve-wracking nights in his hammock, although Patrick was nerveless. When we finally arrived at the rendezvous he smiled and handed me, not the Distinguished Service

Order but a tin of peaches – a rather more welcome present at the time.

During our six-month sojourn in the jungle Patrick had been engaged to marry Julia, and as I can testify had kept faith with her. On our return to the Guards Depot at Pirbright their marriage occurred, attended by myself, Andrew Parker Bowles and two colourful polo players at the time: Harold Bamberg, aviation pioneer still alive aged 104, and Alfie Boyd Gibbins, one of the early property developers. Shortly afterwards a national newspaper published a scurrilous and damaging article revealing Patrick's marriage to the world and contending that he had broken a military code by marrying the divorced wife of a brother officer and arguing that, in a less 'smart' regiment, that would not have been permitted. The upshot of this was that – incredibly – Patrick was required to relinquish his commission and the Army lost one of its outstanding officers. Thereafter Patrick's life was dedicated to the turf. He was a world-class polo player.

4

'COLONELS' IN THE CITY

FTER THE SECOND World War the City began slowly but surely to re-establish itself, and by the 1970s a good living was available to bankers and brokers again. To get to this point a few challenging hurdles needed to be cleared. The first of which was the enquiry into an alleged leak of the Bank Rate increase in 1957 (cf Lord Justice Parker – *Unsung Heroes*). Although it exonerated certain prominent City figures this enquiry, reluctantly instigated by Prime Minister Macmillan under pressure from Harold Wilson, who had heard of its origin from a conversation on a train from Woking between a civil servant, John Pumphrey and the sister of Sir Christopher Chataway who worked in the Conservative Central Office. She gave Pumphrey the impression that she, albeit a lowly secretary, had had advanced knowledge of the change. The charge was taken up gleefully by the Financial Press and the presence of Establishment figures (in particular Lord Kindersley of Lazard and Mr W. J. Keswick of Jardine Matheson) in the witness box at Church House in Westminster enduring rigorous cross-examination by the Attorney General was really the first occasion the public became aware of what we now call 'insider dealing', although all were exonerated.

The second hurdle came with the advent of Mrs Thatcher, who had long disliked the Club-like Public School culture of the 'Old' City. The Stock Exchange was already reeling from charges of restricted practices when 'Big Bang' was launched by her Secretary of State for Trade, Cecil Parkinson. David Kynaston, the City's historian, has related the process of Big Bang accurately and skilfully in volume four of his *The City of London: A Club No More 1945–2000*. He realised how many of the City's Old Guard did not welcome Big Bang and provided an example of the reticence to change as exemplified by the so-called 'Colonels' at Lazard, most of whom had a good war record, were intelligent and charming, but laid-back, spending most afternoons asleep in their offices with their Labradors beside them, or dictating to their secretaries on matters such as the management of their country estates, rather than the affairs of Lazard. It took Ian Fraser and David Verey to whisk the bank into the future where it remains primus inter pares.

Kynaston mentions four 'Colonels': Mark Norman, Daniel Meinertzhagen, A.D. Marris and Christopher (Kit) Dawnay. My impression was that there were at least two other Colonels, Robert Kindersley (son of the Bank Rate Kindersley) and Peter J. Grant. All are alas now dead and the present (4th) Lord Kindersley, although an Etonian and dog lover, actually lives in Toronto! In fact, none of them had ever held the rank of Colonel.

Peter Grant was an interesting man and became a good friend of mine (and indeed of my wife, who herself had direct experience of this younger Colonel whilst heading Lazard's legal department in the 1990s).

Peter's father served in the Caledonians, as did Peter after leaving Eton. He joined the banking house of Edward de Stein, which merged with Lazard in 1960. As a director of Lazard, Chairman of Sun Alliance and of Scottish Hydro amongst many others, Peter radiated Establishment, but he was a very unconventional figure in reality and was the most unpompous of men. He had an impish sense of humour and I had many happy days shooting as his guest up and down the country. He also entertained generously at Boodle's or at Lazard's West End outpost, a flat in Pont Street. It was there that one evening I found myself sitting next to Sir Ian MacGregor, then Mrs Thatcher's favourite businessman (along with Lords King and Hanson).

It so happened that a friend of mine had just backed a new venture, Inter-Rig, the brainchild of Alex Copson, an Anglo-Greek inventor of considerable but impenetrable intelligence. His enthusiasm and energy was such, that after an hour of his company, one needed a week's holiday. This was compounded by the speed of his conversation, of such velocity that I for one had not a clue what he was talking about after he had been in full verbal flight for half an hour. His brains had gone to his head, as Lady Asquith had remarked of F. E. Smith. Nevertheless, he was undeniably inventive, and my friend Richard King and I backed him in various ventures including a notion to bury nuclear waste in the depleted reservoirs of the North Sea oil fields. Inter-Rig, another prospect, was a form of self-stabilising offshore oil rig and sitting next to Sir Ian, who was very agreeable, it occurred to me to explain Copson's concept. Sir Ian enthused about it so, sensing that Lazard may find the capital, I asked Sir Ian to attend a presentation by our ace inventor at the Cluff Oil offices at 58 St James's Street. It remains a recurring nightmare. Alex, in the middle of his rather technically dense presentation, suddenly stopped, pointed to Sir Ian who was clearly nodding off and said: 'What did I just say? You must pay attention you know!' That was the end of that particular fundraising! Alex now lives in America where he thrives, I'm glad to say.

I did visit Lazard occasionally after that; on one occasion for a meeting with Mark Burrell concerning a possible transaction with Premier Oil. There were about twenty of us sitting around a table chaired by Burrell when suddenly the door shot open and an elderly bald suit (who subsequently turned out to be Sir Ian Fraser, the Chairman), thinking it an excess of courtesy to say 'Excuse me' or to introduce himself, simply stood in the doorway and crooked his small finger in the direction of poor Burrell, who practically shot out of the room horizontally. We never saw them again!

David Verey then (about 1990) was appointed as a very young Chief Executive and it was he, I believe, who conceived the admirable idea of dividing BP's Forties field into units, thereby enabling BP to rapidly raise new capital.

By this time Peter Grant had retired from Lazard, leaving only Lord Kindersley and one Labrador of the 'Colonels', although arguably the highly cerebral and unmilitary Tom Manners could be described as an honorary Colonel. The new team of Sir John Nott as Chairman and Verey as Chief Executive flourished.

There is another respect in which Lazard played the pivotal role in my life, although unwittingly. In the 1980s I met and became close to an American girl, Madeleine Hammond, who had married a Saudi Arabian called Alatas. The marriage produced a clever and handsome boy, Mishal, but floundered and Madeleine obtained employment in the corporate finance department at Lazard. Her father Ogden Hammond was the scion of one of the so-called Founding 500 families of the Hudson River. She was also descended from John Cox Stevens, the first Commodore of the New York Yacht Club and founder of the America's Cup.

Madeleine is good-hearted and generous, if a trifle highly strung, and when she started raving about a beautiful Caribbean girl who headed the legal department at Lazard I suggested that she arrange for us all to meet for dinner which she, fatally for our relationship, did, at a restaurant in the King's Road, La Nasa (sadly no more). Things moved quickly and, within a year, Blondel and I were (and still are) married. This caused severe trouble with Madeleine, who showed her contempt for me and the male sex by moving in with another woman!

In the 1980s Peter Grant became very friendly, as did I, with Christopher Moran. Peter quickly grasped that Christopher was a man of considerable ability and intelligence, and Christopher benefited from Peter's advice. Christopher Moran remains a controversial character, in the opinion of a diminishing number. His unpopularity says a lot about what was wrong about this country and many of its institutions in the Thatcher era. From an unprivileged background he managed to secure employment as a clerk in the Lloyd's insurance market. It was not long before he realised the place was a can of worms and represented a lethal combination of incompetence and dishonesty. It was the former which first struck the young clerk, who quickly became aware that he was not only more intelligent than many of the agents, but that the liquid lunches rendered many of them incompetent to conduct business afterwards. Accordingly, he established his own

Agency which opened only for business at 2.30 in the afternoon (and still does). He devised a new form of aviation insurance and was thriving, as indeed were his names. The implosion at Lloyd's has been well documented and Moran was cast as one of the villains by his peers, subjected to star-chamber style vilification and expelled from Lloyd's membership. This was a travesty, as became rapidly apparent when his traducers' true colours were revealed. Ironically Moran was one of the few underwriters who consistently made money legitimately for his names, without having recourse to criminal practices. Peter Grant, John Mathew QC and Lord Goodman were among those who realised how disgracefully he had been treated and sprung to his defence. John Mathew incidentally, the scion of a distinguished legal family, has just died aged ninety-two.

Moran has confounded his tormentors by adding more wealth through property investing and renewable energy in particular, whilst committing a large proportion of his time to his duties as Chairman of the Anglo-Irish Corporation, which led to the conclusion of the Good Friday Agreement, chairing the University College Hospital, guiding the fortunes of the London Symphony Orchestra and as a trustee of the LSO Endowment Trust, having previously chaired the LSE Finance Board.

5

RICHARD KING

I FIRST MET Richard King in November 1959 at a backgammon competition between the St James's Club and Boodle's, which was held at the imposing St James's Clubhouse at 106 Piccadilly, now alas – but probably appropriately – a kindergarten. I recall being part of the St James's team which included Nico Tollenaar, an eighty-year-old Hollander known as the Flying Dutchman because he walked with the aid of two sticks, and an agreeable Greek shipowner, K. Kyriakides, known as Kaos, together with my long-standing friend Paul Irby, a clever and able stockbroker (which he still is). Richard and Captain Robie Uniacke I recall were members of the Boodle's team. A furious row erupted during the evening concerning allegedly unsporting behaviour on our part, and I well remember being impressed by the debating skills of the tall ex-Irish Guards officer, his eyes radiating intelligence and mischief behind those rimless glasses. I quickly realised that there was something very special about this clever, irreverent and very funny barrister, having always valued subversive and self-deprecating humour as far and away the most valuable element in friendships. I was quickly drawn to him, although he was at his wittiest when skirmishing with that other giant of our generation, Paddy Pakenham.

Richard's life was defined institutionally by his beloved Irish Guards, by Sunningdale Golf Club, by Boodle's and by his excursions to ski, and to holiday in Tuscany. But complementary and vital to all of that was wife Vivian and their children. Edward, my godson, told me that he was quite simply the best Dad.

Richard was the most intelligent of our contemporaries, who included a lot of very intelligent people, from Germaine Greer to Barry Humphries, and he could have excelled at virtually anything. However, he resolved not to be a High Court Judge, for example, but to be a businessman. If his manifold ventures sometimes resembled someone crossing a river in full spate – as one boulder crashed he leapt confidently to another – the process was nevertheless always attended by success, most notably his early foray with Colin Forsyth in the unit trust business, and more recently his film production venture, Majestic, and the computer company he founded with Lorenzo Wood and Nat Billington.

I recall the only one which I was involved in was not so successful – an attempt to put some ex-Royal Navy divers to work raising buried treasure in the Caribbean. Our investment of £300,000 led to the recovery of two eighteenth-century nails from offshore Barbados.

There was a financial crisis in the middle of this. I was in Kenya on holiday and needed to speak to Richard urgently. I spent five hours trying to get a phone connection (this was forty years ago) through to Mount Street. Finally, a voice floated through the ether: 'Hello, Nanny speaking.' I hurled the instrument at the wall!

On Richard's sixtieth birthday I gave him lunch at his favourite place, Boodle's. There were about twenty-five of us in the saloon there, including Teddy Goldsmith, Barry Humphries, Ted Dexter, Dolf Mootham, sundry golfing QCs, Irish Guards officers (Docker Boyle in particular) and of course Paddy Pakenham, who was instructed to propose Richard's health. Paddy was wearing his self-designed Irish Guards jacket (he served gallantly at Caterham for six weeks) and I had a feeling of impending doom when Paddy duly rose to his feet and made a witty speech referring to everyone in the room except Richard. This was at the time of the Falklands War, and after his speech he clambered on his chair and gave a spirited rendition of the Argentine National Anthem, which was too much for the misanthropic Secretary who brought the proceedings to a disorderly conclusion by ordering the waiters to remove the Hon. Patrick Pakenham from the building. That sort of thing appealed to Richard, who had a healthy irreverence about him and a delight for the absurder aspects of life.

We seldom savour the quality of our friends until it is too late, but not in the case of Richard, with whom every moment was characterised by that most precious of life's ingredients, laughter, complemented by an unusual kindness and generosity. Whether on the golf course, at the poker table, at Scott's restaurant, around the dining table at 96 Mount Street, where Vivian somehow kept order, or anywhere else – Richard always lifted our spirits.

6

CELEBRITIES

BETWEEN STANDING FOR parliament in 1966 and starting work in earnest as a tyro in the oil business in 1969 I had a brief and tangential contact with various celebrities, which I am sure they will have forgotten although I have not. The first was the lovely chanteuse Françoise Hardy whom my friend Jean-Claude Sauer, a photographer with *Paris Match*, brought over to London for her first and doubtless her last visit. We all had lunch at a basement restaurant, Alexanders, on the corner of King's Road and Alexander Square. This was a favourite haunt of mine, along with Chez Victor in Wardour Street and L'Etoile in Charlotte Street. Alexanders' staff were all Portuguese, including one dear old boy who judged me to be so helpless he not only put sugar in my coffee but also stirred it. Lunch proceeded and, although I was not seated next to Françoise I no doubt gazed at her like a devoted lapdog so after lunch I pressed a note in her hand proposing that we dined at the new 'in' place, Annabel's, just opened by Mark Birley.

To my surprise she materialised at the appointed hour. So surprised was I that I was struck dumb, which scarcely mattered as she spoke not a word of English, whereas my French O Level obtained at Stowe did not provide for the possibility of a coherent conversation with anyone except maybe a French taxi driver. Nevertheless, the evening proceeded with some cordiality not to say amorousness, although the exertions involved in speaking French for five hours led to my imbibing so much French liquid that I rendered myself incoherent in English too. I rate her as one of the most beautiful women I have had the fortune to meet.

Shortly after this I met Mick Jagger and along with Patrick Lichfield and Nicholas Villiers enjoyed a series of dinners with him, mostly at the Clermont Club, then in its heyday. His girlfriend was Jerry Hall and she had a sister, sadly now dead, who came over from Texas to see her and stay with Bryan Ferry, who then had a house somewhere near Orme Square. I asked her to dinner one evening as she was a handsome and friendly girl. I remember little of the dinner other than that she was fairly inebriated when it began and totally plastered by the time it was finished. I managed to insert her into the front seat of my Bentley and during the drive she somehow contrived to slip below the dashboard so that all that was visible were her attractive legs. I arrived at the Ferry house and somehow managed to get her out of the car and into the hall, where I left her lying on the floor. This Bentley was the same one in which I drove Nicholas Villiers from my flat to Claridge's where we were to dine. When we arrived, the top-hatted porter made to open the two front doors. Despite frantic pulling and pushing neither of them would open, leaving Villiers and me with no option but to climb over the fronts seats and out of the back doors. Undignified but very funny and the commissionaire joined in the gaiety – particularly three hours later when, rather the worse for wear, the process had to be repeated in reverse.

When Jagger and Bianca determined to marry I played a modest role in the proceedings. I knew Bianca reasonably well and she was aware that I was renting a bijou house, Le Domaine de la Rose, in Opio in the south of France. The wedding was to be in Saint-Tropez and, as can be imagined, it was going to be quite an occasion. Bianca had to stay separately according to French law and also whilst the marriage 'contract' was being negotiated, so I was approached and asked whether I could lend the house to her. As it happened not only I but also my parents had arranged to be staying there. So Bianca joined the house party and was a beautifully behaved guest, greatly impressing my mother by insisting on making her own bed! My father spent a lot of time in the kitchen playing Gin Rummy with the Jagger chauffeur. That was in 1971 and other than the occasional glimpse of Mick at Lord's I have not seen either of them since.

The two celebrity collectors I have known better than any celebrity were Geoffrey Keating and David Tang. Geoffrey, I have written about before. He was outrageous but certainly not a bore. Indeed, I think he was one of the more interesting characters I have known. His career had included a spell advising Field Marshal Montgomery on how to communicate with the press and indeed with his soldiers as although a military genius he was a cold fish. Geoffrey, although armed only with a camera, was always in the thick of the battles in North Africa and was awarded the Military Cross.

Geoffrey was also possessed of a warm personality and a kind heart as I appreciated when

I accompanied him to Marrakesh to see Field Marshal Auchinleck. Geoffrey had known the Field Marshal in his North African soldiering days, and he understood that the 'Auk' was living in poverty in Marrakesh so we resolved to visit him and see what could be done. I brought a reluctant Chinese girl with me. It poured with rain throughout the three-day trip, which Geoffrey and I spent happily playing backgammon. Our visit to the Field Marshal was arranged to occur in a coffee house and Geoffrey undertook to collect him and meet me and the girl. Alas the distinguished Field Marshal was not only practically destitute but was also seemingly suffering from dementia and made practically no sense at all. Geoffrey (and I) were enraged that this distinguished soldier had been abandoned and on our return Geoffrey raised Cain about this until, to his credit, Denis Healey, then Minister of Defence, arranged for the Auk to have a batman and a car at his disposal. He died shortly after our visit in March 1981. Another of our most distinguished and revered soldiers, Field Marshal Alanbrooke, having directed our military strategy throughout the Second World War, was also so impoverished in retirement that he was forced to sell his beloved collection of bird books to make ends meet.

Geoffrey used to have legendary lunches at a round table in his house in Three King's Yard opposite the side entrance of Claridge's. At one of these the guests were John le Carré, Sir Maurice Oldfield and myself. Oldfield was at the time 'C', the head of MI6. Geoffrey had known him from when he was a Lieutenant Colonel in Military Intelligence in North Africa. I cannot remember the purpose of the lunch, but I expect it was to furnish le Carré with some colour for his current book. Oldfield bore a striking resemblance to Alec Guinness's Smiley in *Tinker, Tailor, Soldier, Spy*. He was from a Derbyshire farming family and proudly retained his North Country accent. It emerged towards the end of his career that he was homosexual but he was cleared of compromising security and was reemployed in Northern Ireland where he was falsely accused by credulous police during the Operation Midland affair of sexual irregularities at the Elm Guest House. Again, he was exonerated but had died aged sixty-five in 1981.

David Tang had a more predatory celebrity fixation; indeed one began to feel that all his friends were celebrities. This was not the case, as I can testify. I have in front of me his clever book *Rules for Modern Life*, which he inscribed for me as 'being for many years my mentor'. This, in the light of events which have surfaced since his early death, is a somewhat back-handed compliment! Nevertheless, he was really an extraordinary man possessed of exceptional gifts but also of two fatal flaws. He was cultured (concert standard pianist), entrepreneurial, creative, and great fun. His flaws were a disarming but ultimately destructive obsession to be not only a celebrity but also to be the peer of the grandest in the land. Keeping up with the Marlboroughs, the Keswicks and the Northumberlands was beyond his financial abilities and led to his second flaw, gambling, which merely compounded the problem, leaving him to adopt less acceptable tactics. The scale of his (unsuccessful) gambling can be gauged from the following. I was chatting to the head waiter of one of the clubs to which I belong. He had only just been appointed and he told me that previously he had been a croupier at a casino in Curzon Street, where he said he recalled seeing me dining occasionally with 'Sir David'. The waiter then revealed that he had once been at the receiving end of a £90,000 tip from David, with which he bought himself a house! Unfortunately, it emerged after David's death that for many years he had been plundering the assets of various companies without the knowledge of the shareholders in order to fund his mythomaniacal life. The intense pressure of sustaining this systematic fraud for twenty years must have been terrible and presumably hastened his death.

7

A Weekend with Sir Vivyan Naylor-Leyland

I N THE 1960s I was very friendly with Michael Pearson (now Lord Cowdray). Michael was always a generous friend and one week in October 1967 I was invited to join him for a cruise up the Dardanelles to Istanbul in his yacht appropriately named *The Hedonist*. This I was particularly keen to do as my uncle was killed at Gallipoli and I wished to visit his grave. The party, other than Michael, included Rupert Deen (a genial and decidedly underpowered man about town), myself and Sir Vivyan Naylor-Leyland, previously unknown to me.

Vivyan was a tall hatchet-faced and handsome fellow, with whom I had something in common since he had also been a Grenadier. He had a fearsome reputation for losing his temper in spectacular fashion, often without warning – I suppose he was what we now call bipolar. He was about twenty years older than the rest of us and we treated him with some caution. As I recall he had two leading conversational topics: horses (in favour) and the tax man (against). In fact, avoiding tax became an obsession, eventually leading to him oscillating between Jersey and the Caribbean. This was a shame because he was blessed with a handsome property, the Nantclwyd Estate in Denbighshire. His fortune was derived from Welsh coal mining.

As the cruise continued there was no evidence of Vivyan's legendary rages. Quite the reverse in fact and by the time *The Hedonist* deposited us in Istanbul, Vivyan and I had become firm friends. At this time, I had achieved some mild celebrity (short-lived) as a result of my exertions in the pursuit of North Sea oil. However, I was still feeling my way socially and remained primarily an urban animal, unsure of myself away from my parents' world of golf and bridge. In fact, other than running, I do not recall that I was possessed of any sporting talent at all. However, I was unsurprised shortly after the conclusion of our Aegean Idyll to be invited to spend a shooting weekend at Nantclwyd.

I had a flat in Eaton Square – number 18 – a Bentley, some Savile Row suits, one oil painting and not much else. So, I bought a twelve-bore shotgun, two cashmere pullovers and some cartridges. I thought one box would do.

London to Nantclwyd was quite a hack in those pre-motorway days but I arrived promptly and met my fellow guests: two very grand and very agreeable contemporaries of Vivyan, Charlie Smith-Ryland and Johnny Macdonald-Buchanan. There was also a nice Greek gentleman called Mavroleon who vanished before the shoot the following morning (it turned out that he was so overwhelmed by the occasion that he rang his office and got them to send a telegram saying his wife was ill).

There was no sign of Vivyan when I arrived and my new friends advised me that Vivyan had got married again that very morning in a Registry Office in London to a girl with the unlikely (but necessarily double-barrelled) name of Starr Anker-Simmons. I went to change for dinner and we assembled in the drawing room. I suddenly became aware of the other, darker, Vivyan: he was manifestly very angry about something and the brand new (and very nice and attractive) Lady Naylor-Leyland was emitting signs of anxiety.

We went into the dining room, where she was next to me. I discovered that she was South African although of Danish origin and had met her new husband on the hunting field. (She certainly had a 'good seat'.) After dinner the volcanic Vivyan ordained that we men should play backgammon and Starr, the solitary girl, went off to bed. Having spent six years in the Army, backgammon was one of my few competencies and I was alarmed at the prospect of defeating Sir Volatile. I therefore tried to lose ... and the more I tried to lose, the more I won. After an uninterrupted run of six wins the evening concluded with a crash – the backgammon board being swept from the table by my host.

I retired to bed in a state of some anxiety. I had never shot anywhere before, except with my eighty-year-old friend Sir John Dixon around a bog in Cheshire, where the bag never reached double figures.

Eventually morning came. I was duly placed by Vivyan in readiness for the first drive. The birds began to swarm over my head and by the end of it I had shot one pheasant and used up all my cartridges. It was too late to follow Mr Mavroleon's lead and vanish so I owned up to my neighbour Charlie Smith-Ryland. At this point Sir Vivyan rode up on his horse wearing a cloak and looking very menacing.

'Vivyan,' Charlie said, 'Algy has run out of cartridges.'

Wedding in Hong Kong, 1993, with David C. T. Lie, son of a
Nationalist General and member of the Chinese politburo.

Trooping the Colour: Blondel,
Harry and Philip, 2001.

Blondel with President Jerry Rawlings
and his wife Nana, in Ghana.

New York friends: Bobby Power, Captain of the Yale Polo team 1959; Louis Pemberton and wife Suzanne (photo by Katrina Thomas).

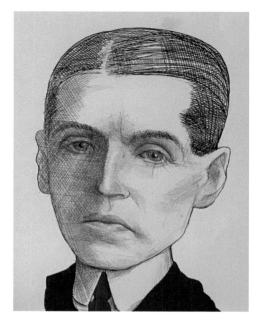

The remarkable F. E. Smith, as seen by Spy and Springs.

Gdsn. J. Dale,   R. Laing,   M. Langton,   P. Sheehy,   P. Kenworthy-Browne,   I Macdonald
dsn. K. Rose,   The Earl of Breckn
     The Hon. R. Erskine,   M. Scott.   A. Tennant,   P. Houison-Craufurd,   The Hon. S. Stuart,   J. Shakespeare,   M. Dormer,   R. Mayfield
a. The Viscount Stormont,   Sgt. J. McLoughlin,   SGT. A. MOSELEY,   Capt. A. B. Pemberton,   Td.S. C. Stephens,   Sgt. L. Gilham,   Gds. R. St. G. Calvocor
                              (W. T. Instr.)   (Squad Instr.)   (Tactics Instr.)

Patrick Sheehy, centre back row.

Opposite: Three Captains and one wife. Clockwise from top right: Julia
Williamson (with Andrew Parker Bowles), Darel Carey (with Annabel Elliot),
Sir Nicholas Nuttall, Lord Patrick Beresford.

Charlie Smith-Ryland and his daughter Sarah (now Mrs Henry Strutt).

Starr Anker-Simmons, then Naylor-Leyland and now Harper.

Nantclwyd Hall, domain of Sir Vivyan Naylor-Leyland.

The lovely chanteuse
Françoise Hardy.

Bianca Jagger.

Curraghmore, domain of
the Marquess of Waterford.

David Tang.

Hong Kong Harbour.

Captain Carey on the left in brown suit. David Bailey snapping Patrick Lichfield, 1969. Image by lesser photographer A. Cluff.

Below R: Henry Keswick, Andrew Devonshire, Mark Birley.

Richard King.

Lunch at the Berry house at Sologne, near Orléans. L to R: Blondel, William Berry, the King of Serbia, AC, Charlie Cluff, Eleonore Berry, Alexander Berry.

A forgotten classic: peerless travel writing and an original study of melancholy.

Field Marshal Auchinleck – the 'Auk'.

Harold Nicolson, Vita Sackville-West, Rosamund Grosvenor and Lionel Sackville-West in 1913.

'Oh that's OK, he can get some more from his cartridge bag,' replied Vivyan.

'No Vivyan, he doesn't have any more, nor does he have a cartridge bag, but I shall lend him mine,' which he kindly did. At this point I was expecting some kind of eruption from Vivyan (as Charlie had warned me to expect), whereas to everyone's amazement he behaved as if it were perfectly normal to run out of cartridges after the first drive, and my nervous breakdown was deferred. The rest of the weekend was without incident.

Soon after, Vivyan became a tax exile in the Bahamas and I never saw him again. He divorced Starr in 1975, married again and died in 1987. Curiously my ally, Charlie Smith-Ryland, became a friend until his untimely death after an unselfish life of public service, and his daughter Sarah, beautiful, high-spirited and ever interested, became a good friend too. She married Henry Strutt, with whom I have been happily shooting at his estate in Suffolk for thirty years and where I am never seen without at least two cartridge bags. Nantclwyd continues in the ownership of the Naylor-Leyland family, Vivyan's son being the current proprietor. His mother, Vivyan's first wife, Elizabeth Anne, was a very soignée and knowledgeable adornment on the staff of Christie's for many years before marrying a dashing Tory MP.

8

MARQUESS OF WATERFORD

STAYING WITH THE Marquess of Waterford, always known as Tyrone, at Curraghmore for a day's shooting, as my wife and I did for many years, was a privilege, but there was also a curious sense that, on arrival, one had stepped back a hundred years into the past. We would fly to Cork weighed down with guns and ammunition, hire a car and set off to Portlaw where the magnificent estate of Curraghmore is located. This in itself was something of a challenge as one got the impression that all the street signs had been re-set to point in the wrong direction, as had been the case in invasion-threatened Britain during the Second World War (on that occasion to confound the enemy). Arriving at dusk at Curraghmore was a surreal experience, the house soaring above (so dramatic is the first sight of the house that, during the Troubles, a mob intent on setting it on fire were so transfixed by the huge crucifix on the roof illuminated by a full moon that they ran for their lives).

Ascending the steps past a massive open fire there is a sign surrounded by dozens of bottles of sundry spirits which reads: 'Sportsmen will assemble at 8.15am for briefing'. Then through massive doors and into the elegant hallway where, assisted by Basil, the South African butler, one ascends the staircase as if climbing a mountain. The temperature drops remorselessly until one arrives in a massive bedroom 'heated' by a one-bar electric fire, timed to operate for two hours as one changes for dinner. On one particular year I apprehended another guest, Harry Hambleden, in the act of removing the only blanket from our bed!

Downstairs for drinks before dinner in a sitting room where the guests assemble, greeted by Tyrone in velvet smoking jacket and his ethereal and, I suspect, long-suffering wife Caroline, who has largely switched her allegiance from the human race to the four-legged fraternity. On the walls there are striking modern portraits of Beresfords by de László and somewhere a skilful study of Tyrone and his brother Patrick in hunting costume by Simon Elwes. The guests nearly always included the splendid Captain Fergus Sutherland with the original poached-egg eyes, who had mysteriously lost a foot during the Korean War. Fergie was a crack shot and blessed with a benign and cheerful disposition.

Dinner involved another drop in temperature as one filed down a freezing corridor to the dining room, past a huge painting of a Royal Navy ship on the Nile, captained by Admiral Charles Beresford, one of Tyrone's distinguished antecedents (who nearly married an exotic Tahitian lady). This dining room, panelled and intimate, was happily charged with innumerable bottles of wine and eventually we all ascended the peak to our bedrooms in a haze of alcohol prior to getting dressed before going to bed, it by this time being 10 degrees colder in the house than outside!

At 7am the Marquess patrolled the staircase ringing a fire bell to rally the sportsmen to breakfast in the small dining room, then out into the park for the shoot in which there are trees of majesty and history such as I had never before seen. Tyrone in command and at the wheel of a vehicle which could only have been made in Ireland. His delightful son James, I suspect, handled most of the organisation of the day and Caroline was the Mistress of the Pickers-Up with her kennel of dogs. Back in the house for lunch in an enormous dining room dominated by a huge bust of the Duke of Wellington; my wife was always seated on Tyrone's right and the fare was Irish stew followed by a gigantic stilton. After this the sportsmen set off for an afternoon of more shooting before a massive tea and the trip back to Cork, Gatwick and Westminster.

Tyrone, an original if ever there was one, is now dead and his eldest son, also Tyrone, is now the Marquess and has I gather edged the estate into the twenty-first century.

9

THE 1ˢᵀ EARL OF BIRKENHEAD: F. E. SMITH

F. E., AS he was always known, is one of the outstanding characters of the twentieth century although strangely forgotten today. Had he lived during the Second World War he would undoubtedly have served in the War Cabinet, having previously been Churchill's closest confidant. It has always surprised me that, notwithstanding holding high office including Secretary of State for India and Lord Chancellor, there is no public monument to him anywhere in this country, but then there is no monument in Parliament Square to William Pitt, Robert Walpole or Charles James Fox, although there is to Gandhi and Mandela.

I had an unusual experience whilst staying with my friend Nicholas Berry, F. E.'s grandson, who for twenty years rented his distinguished kinsman's house in Charlton in Oxfordshire. After dinner I was sitting alone in F. E.'s famous library, and I had just lit a cigar whilst I reflected on the history of that room when there was a crash, a window shattered. Someone had thrown a large brick through it! There was no message attached to the brick to indicate for whom it was intended, and the episode remains a mystery.

The house is in fact three village houses in one and was the much-loved residence of F. E. for many years.

F. E. is remembered now chiefly for his aperçus and his forensic skill in court. As an example of the latter, when at the Liverpool Bar he was retained by the local bus company to resist a suit for damages instituted by the indigent parents of a youth who claimed he was unable to use his left arm as a result of falling off an 'omnibus'. The child is produced in court.

'How high can you lift your arm since the accident?' F. E. solicitously enquired.

The youth grimaced as he raised his arm painfully to his waist.

'I see' said F. E., '... and can you show us how high you could raise it before the unfortunate accident?'

The youth's arm shot up shoulder high!

F. E.'s wit could be cruel as well as funny. Winston Churchill once asked F. E. in the presence of F. E.'s wife Margaret, what he judged to be the chief milestones in his life? F. E. replied: when I was called to the bar, when I took silk and when I became Lord Chancellor.

'What about our marriage?' Margaret intervened.

F. E. replied, 'Winston said milestones, not millstones!'

F. E. was a most attractive individual physically. Six foot three inches tall, thick black hair, cigar clasped in position, immaculate morning dress and cane in hand. Alas there was always a glass of alcohol in his other hand! The medical reason he died aged fifty-eight was cirrhosis of the liver, and his detractors charged him with corroding many of his son's fellow undergraduates with alcoholism as a result of the Herculean binges over which he presided at Charlton during the 1920s.

Charlton itself is his creation: the three tennis courts, the stables and above all the library, in which I was sitting when my unknown assailant hurled a brick through the window. F. E. was a dedicated bibliophile and a large part of his collection was housed at his substantial London residence, 32 Grosvenor Gardens. On one occasion F. E. had cause to check into an hotel and noticed the previous entry in the

Register read: 'The Lochiel and Mrs Cameron', moving F. E. to inscribe '32 Grosvenor Gardens and Mrs Smith'.

He really belonged to the eighteenth century where he would have been at one with Pitt and Fox. Alas his title expired when his teetotal bachelor grandson, Robin Birkenhead, had a heart attack on one of the three tennis courts at Charlton. Ironically, he had rejected alcohol in favour of copious draughts of black coffee, which was what killed him, aged thirty-eight. He had just published a scholarly biography of Wilberforce, and seemed set for a distinguished literary career. He had the eccentric tendency to collect anything cast in the form of an elephant, and his memorial above the tennis courts at Charlton is a Portland-stone bench with two elephant profiles at either end.

10

SIX WYKEHAMISTS

THE APPOINTMENT OF Rishi Sunak as Chancellor of the Exchequer in February 2020 was the first time that a Wykehamist has occupied that important office of State since Sir Stafford Cripps in the post-War Attlee Administration. Sunak's rise affirms that this venerable college retains its preeminent place at the apex of the British educational system.

I have been fortunate to know six Wykehamists for many years – two of whom, Jasper Larken and Charles Black, are dead. However, Bobby Power, David Hunter, David Davies and Simon Courtauld all continue to thrive. With Jasper, I used to own an elegant ketch, *Linette*, which we moored on the Hamble for five years from 1962, until Jasper went to live in New York, where he made an enduring marriage to Caroline Little, the daughter of the *New York Times* theatre critic and of a Danish mother, related to the distinguished Raben family.

Charles Black died too young and was mourned by a wide circle of friends. After Winchester he served in the Scots Guards before assuming the mantle of Chief Executive of the family business, A. & C. Black, the publishers of, in particular, *Who's Who*. He married the striking and formidable Melanie, elder daughter of Sir Denys Colquhoun Flowerdew Lowson, 1st Baronet. Sir Denys was a highly controversial and financially adept individual who, although thirty-three when the War began, remained at the heart of the City of London and of various Livery Companies and Masonic Lodges, culminating in serving as Lord Mayor from 1950–51, the year of the Festival of Britain. In those days the Lord Mayor automatically became a Baronet, which Lowson did at the age of forty-five. He sat at the centre of a web of investment trusts and trading companies, which he ran with complete disregard for the requirements of what we now call corporate governance. Some of these companies – such as the Anglo-Thai Corporation – were conspicuously successful despite Sir Denys's tendency to conflate his affairs with those of the shareholders, to the disadvantage of the latter. The authorities began to move against him after Harold Wincott, the crusading editor of the *Investors Chronicle*, in one of the first examples of investigative financial journalism, launched a probe into his affairs. He adroitly preempted the investigation by dying.

Charles and Melanie Black were both gifted with unusual good looks, intelligence and in Charles's case sporting prowess. In particular he was an excellent if unorthodox golfer and their lives were primarily defined by activities at the Royal St George's Golf Club at Sandwich, and for many years they owned a house in the Bay. Charles's business and other dealings were characterised by absolute integrity. Following an accident which befell their son, he became much concerned about the future of the family business and eventually took the difficult decision to sell it and effectively retired at an early age. Sandwich Bay in the 1970s and 1980s was home to a thriving colony of rich and successful businessmen, many of whom had been contemporaries of Charles's in the Brigade of Guards, or as in the case of David Hunter at Winchester. Hunter was the son of a Sandwich Bay habitué, Jock Hunter, the Senior Partner of L. Messel, one of the leading pre-Big Bang banking firms. Well into his eighties, David continues to work in the City respected by investors and feared by indigent executives. His intimidating manner belies an unusual degree of kindness and generosity, particularly to military charities.

***

Jasper Larken had a good mind and a ready wit. Tall and ginger, he was the son and grandson of Naval officers. His father, Wyatt, was a memorable figure and I can see him vividly in the drawing room of their house in Chester Square in the 1960s – bow tie, monocle and vodka & tonic, looking exactly as Ian Fleming portrayed M in the early Bond novels.

Jasper joined the Grenadiers after Winchester and was a popular officer. He elected to seek his fortune in New York from 1966 and became an investment banker on Wall Street, where – and at the Racquet Club – his acid wit rendered him welcome. Returning to the UK with Caroline, he was afflicted with a mysterious ailment which excluded him from work and rendered his existence difficult, deprived of most food and all alcohol. It was a form of cancer and finally killed him.

***

Bobby Power, of Anglo-Irish extraction, went on to Yale from Winchester although he remains a lifelong friend of mine and of the other Wykehamists mentioned here. He elected to remain in New York where tragically his first (French) wife, Elianne, choked to death in their apartment whilst he was out walking their dog. He was devastated by this but valiantly pressed on with his career on Wall Street, which was complemented by an outstanding record of sporting achievement, as recorded on the rolls of honour on the walls of the Racquet and Tennis Club. Tennis, racquets, snooker, golf … he excelled at them all, but being the least boastful of men none would be aware of it. He married again very happily and now lives in Vermont.

David Davies is the fifth Wykehamist I have known, and he and I are the same age. After Winchester he was an exhibitioner at New College Oxford after which he went to Harvard on the first of a series of leaps and bounds. Beginning with five years at Chase Manhattan and including senior management roles at the property company MEPC, Hill Samuel Bank, Hongkong Land, Johnson Matthey and others. As he moved from one to the other, he was able to exercise options and enrich himself. There are many dimensions to David and his interests in opera and heritage (in particular, Irish Georgian architecture, following his purchase of Abbey Leix, one of Ireland's foremost houses) render him a man of consequence. It would be wrong to conclude without testifying to his healthy, successful and continuous interest in the opposite sex.

***

When I owned *The Spectator* magazine the deputy editor was another Wykehamist, Simon Courtauld, or 'Lavish McTavish', to use his mysterious sobriquet. In those days we had an uneasy relationship, helped by my decision to fire the feckless editor who was spending my money contemptuously. Simon resigned in solidarity at this difficult point in the affairs of the magazine. However, eventually he returned to the fold and we became and remain good friends. A barrister, Simon used to read the magazine for libel which he did competently, although as luck would have it he was on holiday when Taki filed the fateful article 'D Gay Day', about the egregious socialite Mrs Marcie-Rivière. As mentioned by Taki in the foreword to this volume, that landed us up in front of Mr Justice Otton with very expensive consequences.

When Conrad Black became *The Spectator*'s proprietor, Kimberly Fortier and I persuaded him that it was time for a history of the magazine to be written. This Simon was selected to write and he produced a most useful and readable effort, *To Convey Intelligence: The Spectator 1928–98*. I subsequently suggested to him that a life of Derek Jackson should be written and this he did. Although Jackson was in many ways a disagreeable, not to say obnoxious, man, he was also brave and clever and his tendency to marry multiple times to formidable women renders his life of some sociological and historic interest, which Simon skilfully brings out. Amongst his wives was Janetta Woolley, daughter of the Reverend Herbert Woolley VC MC. Janetta also married five times and turned many distinguished heads. Her daughter, Rose, now lives at Long Crichel House, which was inhabited by a number of gay intellectuals, as described in a recent book.

Simon's real interest is in Spain, about which he has written a number of books, and in gardening; he was for three years in the 1980s editor of *The Field*.

***

I suppose these Wykehamists will have attended the school between 1953 and 1958, during which time it clearly maintained the highest standards. The school was hit by intermittent problems during the last twenty years so it is cheering that one of its alumni now occupies one of the three most powerful offices of State, the Chancellor of the Exchequer.

11

SIR PATRICK SHEEHY

PATRICK SHEEHY – Pat to his many friends
– was one of the commercial giants of
the twentieth century, but also a man of
many parts who unselfishly contributed greatly
to the public good.

Pat was a modest man but of terrifying aspect
to those who had the misfortune not to know
him. Those who did were aware that behind
that intimidating exterior there obtained a
heart of gold. His appearance conformed to the
popular notion of a capitalist, but that appearance was very misleading. His voice too could
be intimidating, particularly his tendency
to end his sentences with an interrogatory
grunt! His views were not necessarily allied
to the mainstream, but he was a scourge of
self-importance.

Pat's professional life was devoted to British
American Tobacco, which he joined from
National Service in the Irish Guards. Eventually

he became Chief Executive and subsequently the company Chairman. Under his leadership the company flourished and he set the scene for its transformation into BAT Industries. I will go as far as to say that BAT owes its continued existence to Pat, for in 1989 certain rich and colourful individuals conceived the idea of breaking BAT up, and selling off the non-tobacco side. I assume they had done their arithmetical homework, but they had fatefully neglected to do their Sheehy homework, and completely underestimated the company's leader. They had misread him as a golfing nonentity who would be no match for their wiliness and wealth. In fact, Pat, with his small team (including Michael Prideaux), ran rings around the so-called Hoylake Consortium who realised, all too late, that they had stirred the lion in his cage. And the lion was not only highly intelligent but was also truly formidable. That adjective, formidable, was indeed the element that radiated from Pat, whether at the helm of BAT or sitting in his favourite chair by the bar at the Royal St George's Golf Club.

He loved that club dearly and inevitably became one of its distinguished Captains. In 1963 I sat next to Ian Fleming at a backgammon dinner in Boodle's, and he memorably told me how fatigued he was with all his celebrity, which he never wanted.

'Well, what did you want?' I rather importunately asked.

'To be the Captain of the Royal St George's Golf Club' was the astonishing reply.

When Fleming died in Canterbury hospital, after his final round of golf at the Royal St George's, he was the Captain Elect of the club. So, when Pat in his turn became Captain, I sent him a number of photographs of Bobby Sweeney and of Ian Fleming. To my surprise Pat returned the one of Ian Fleming. 'Fleming never quite made it,' he explained, when next I saw him. So Fleming's photograph never qualified to join the rows of Old Etonian Stockbrokers on the walls of the Clubhouse.

Pat and I met in 1970, just over fifty years ago, and although I am not Irish, Roman Catholic, a golfer or a smoker we became firm friends, largely I think because we did have one important element in common – humour. I feel melancholy knowing that we shall not hear that laugh again, reminiscent of a hand grenade exploding! We were both good trenchermen too, and I see him vividly now in my mind's eye tucking his napkin into his collar before attacking a dozen oysters at Wiltons Restaurant.

We went all over the place together, including his beloved Africa. We had one memorable trip to Johannesburg to meet with executives from Anglo American. We arrived very early in the morning and I retired to bed until lunchtime, whilst Pat went straight to the Johannesburg Country Club to play eighteen holes of golf. The next morning, we arrived for our meeting at 44 Main Street, and I noticed a happy smile playing on his face during the meeting. It was only when we were leaving the building that I realised the cause of the smile: the security guard on our arrival had some difficulty with my name and had written not Mr Algy but Ugly Cluff on my security card.

I asked Pat to join the boards of various oil and mining companies with which I was associated in those days, and his probity and common sense helped me enormously. The respect I had for Pat was the best discipline I could have wished for.

I also asked him to join me, Norman Tebbit, Christopher Fildes and John King of British Airways on the Board of *The Spectator*, where he was a wise and congenial presence for many years. There was no great love lost between John King and Pat, which led to an entertaining degree of sulphur around the table for the rest of us. Our Board meetings were held at my office in St James's and afterwards we frequently adjourned to Brooks's Club. However, the first occasion that Frank Johnson, not an easy man, attended the Board meeting as editor was particularly memorable. There was no formal dinner planned so Pat and I had agreed to repair to Wiltons afterwards. Johnson, as editor, made it clear that he had no time for the Board's views (we eventually sacked him) and kept on ostentatiously consulting his watch, as if he had something more important to do, so, as a matter of courtesy, I sped the meeting along. After the meeting Pat and I arrived at Wiltons where, having dinner at the next table on his own, and on *The Spectator*, was Frank Johnson! One of the Editors was none other than our present Prime Minister, who reminded me recently that the Board had twice moved to reduce his salary by 20 per cent, a move successfully and characteristically resisted by Pat. Our future Prime Minister's mortgage was safe!

Now that Pat has alas joined the concourse in the sky, we have lost a giant among our contemporaries. A serious and good man who was conspicuously successful, but also a human being without a trace of self-importance. There was nothing phoney about Pat, and above all he lived a wonderful family life with his wife Jill, his staunch although independent consort through fifty-five years of marriage. He was very much a family man, consonant with his deep Roman Catholic ethic, and he was very close to his children Michael and Joanna and his grandchildren. I happily recall all those shared adventures, whether in the boardroom, dining room or on the golf course. He will always remain vividly etched in my mind's eye.

12

How Right They Were

O NE EVENING IN July 1994 there occurred a dinner party at 26 Middle Gap Road, halfway up the prestigious peak in Hong Kong. Our host was David Davies, then Chief Executive of Hongkong Land, and his guests were Simon Murray, then Chief Executive of Hutchison Whampoa, David Tang, entrepreneur and indefatigable worker for charity, and me. More importantly there were four prominent Hong Kong Chinese businessmen, all in their prime. The catalyst for the dinner was the growing anxiety amongst our Chinese friends that the ongoing negotiations with the Communist Chinese had not been preceded by any consultation with the Hong Kong Chinese Community about how the Foreign Office should conduct these negotiations. This at best was discourteous and at worst mistaken.

Our Chinese friends were of the view that,

because the Chinese Communists were not to be trusted on any level, Herculean efforts should have been made to extend the British lease on Hong Kong. They believed that the current British approach was essentially unsophisticated, and since China at that point in time was chronically short of foreign exchange, they would have responded favourably to the suggestion of an extension to the lease provided it was accompanied by a rental measured in billions of dollars. Our Hong Kong friends were angry that the Foreign Office concern was to dispose of a political problem as rapidly as possible.

The negotiations had originally been triggered at a routine meeting between Hong Kong's Governor, Murray MacLehose, and the Chinese leadership in Beijing. MacLehose had come under great pressure from the Hong Kong bankers to raise the question of the provision of mortgages beyond 1997. MacLehose tabled this at the end of the meeting and without warning. The Chinese sensed they were being subject to a trick and made it crystal clear that come what may the New Territories (the leasehold area as opposed to the freehold area of Hong Kong Island) should revert to China in 1997. These anxieties were liberated at the

Middle Gap Road dinner, assisted by David Davies's excellent wine cellar. All four of us were shocked and disturbed by the violence of the views articulated that evening. We resolved to do something about it. Thus was formed the Anglo-Hong Kong Trust, dedicated to alerting those interested to the untrustworthy characteristics of the Chinese Communists, as well as the need for Britain to adopt a much more benign attitude to the allocation of British passports to Hong Kong citizens.

We laboured with twenty other Chinese friends to achieve our objective, although we were often treated with some disdain by the British Sinophile 'expats'. We arranged numerous events, from a dinner at Lancaster House in London to one on the Royal Yacht in Hong Kong. The driving force amongst us was undoubtedly David Tang. Although the Trust failed in its primary objective of alerting the British officials to the untrustworthiness of the Chinese leadership, it did lead to some attention being paid to the issuance of passports and it eventually led to the foundation of Hong Kong's first Chair of Business Studies at Hong Kong University (thanks to the generosity of Dickson Poon) as well as to the establishment on various housing projects of English Language

Schools (thanks to the generosity of the Swire business empire). Alongside his work with the late Sir Ronald Grierson for cancer charities, David Tang has left an important legacy that cannot be extirpated by subsequent events.

It gives me no pleasure to record how right our Hong Kong friends were proved to be; we now see China increasingly behaving in a sinister manner in no way consonant with the terms or the spirit of the 1997 Agreement.

There was no more melancholy sign of the total failure of the British objectives than the sight of the Chinese delegation at the handover ceremony turning their backs as Prince Charles steamed out of Hong Kong on the Royal Yacht for the last time.

13

THE FAILURES OF THE CITY SYSTEM

AMONGST THE FAILURES of the City system is what I would call 'the tyranny of the share price'. This is the fund manager's insistence on performance and in particular news flow. It renders previously normal executives partially deranged in their anxiety to push the share price up whilst endeavouring to manage the company for the long-term benefit of the employees and the fiscus, rather than for the short-term satisfaction of the fund manager. My experience of the latter is that most of us would be no worse off by managing our own money and reading the *Daily Mail* City page every day – which is what the fund managers do! It did lead, however, to some amusing situations. I had a friend, Derek Williams, who was the Chief Executive of a small mining company, Charterhall. One day he was asked to lunch at a small but lively broking firm – Fiske & Co.

I was there too. Fiske only had three partners: the Marquess of Ailesbury (invisible, sleeping), Simon Wharmby and Frank Watts, two cheerful and smart individuals. Lunch proceeded with a presentation by Derek about the manifold qualities of the Charterhall company's assets. At some point during this arresting exposition Simon said – setting a trap – 'What's your share price now, Derek?'

'You know Simon, I am not distracted by the share price. I just get on and work 24/7 for the company.'

'It's 10 ½,' said Frank Watts.

'No, it's not, it's 11 ¼,' Derek haplessly snapped back.

Much laughter ensued. I may say I was just as much a culprit as Derek. One weekend my good friend Paddy Pakenham, who pointedly had just given me a copy of 'Shareholders' Rights' for Christmas, drew my attention to a press article questioning whether the Cluff Oil share price overvalued the company's assets. I replied rather sharply, which prompted the following ditty on a postcard:

There was a young fellow called Cluff
Whose critics accused him of puff
'But my shares never falter
They are the rock of Gibraltar'
He replied off the cuff in a huff.

14

THE COMMONWEALTH CONNECTION

FOR A NUMBER of years, I had the misfortune to serve as a Trustee of the Commonwealth Institute, a completely ineffectual organisation dedicated to the promotion of the Commonwealth, which had been wilting in the face of Tony Blair's obsession with Europe. The Institute was run by a Director General who reported to a Board of Trustees. The two Directors General during my tenure were Stephen Cox and David French, both thoroughly decent and competent, but lacking any real direction from the Trustees. The Institute building (now happily flourishing as the Design Centre) was, according to your taste, either the second-most-important twentieth-century building in London ... or a complete eyesore. I was inclined to the latter persuasion: it was so badly designed as to render current occupation and use otiose. The

Trustees' problems were compounded by the deterioration of the building and the lack of money to do anything about it.

In the middle of all this it was necessary to find a new Director General. Headhunters were appointed who duly came up with a shortlist and a selection of the Trustees (who included all the High Commissioners based in London) were invited to scrutinise the shortlist and interview the candidates. I was included as a member of the panel, along with a representative of the Foreign Office. Among the interviewees was a rather elegant lady in twin-set and pearls whose CV had struck me as I read it through the previous evening. Amongst her achievements was an impressive period in the Army, where she had reached the rank of Lieutenant Colonel. I asked my wife to read it through too and she said that there was something odd about the handwriting. I must say that I was impressed by the candidate's conduct at the interview, but I chose to support a more conventional male candidate. In this I was firmly in the minority. The Chairman, Sir David Thompson, then called in the headhunter and advised him that the elegant lady candidate was the preferred if not unanimous choice of the Trustees. At this point the headhunter cleared his throat and said that we made a wise choice in his opinion but that, before she was called in, he felt that we should know that she was a transsexual. Well in this respect she had caught us unawares.

One of the High Commissioners enquired: 'What is a transsexual?'

'No, no, no!' he said, when the man from the Foreign Office had explained clearly.

In the event the job – in some respects a poisoned chalice – went to the more conventional candidate for whom I had voted. Today the transsexual would have been appointed with acclaim. Fortunately this rejection, which would now be viewed as discriminatory, in no way damaged her subsequent distinguished career!

15

PORTRAITS

A MONGST THE MOST precious volumes in my library is the *Dictionary of National Biography* together with its numerous supplements. It is a must for the scholar, the historian and those like myself who are just interested in interesting people. Until recently the entries often concluded with the information that an oil painting of this particular subject was in the possession of the family or a university or a national art gallery, and went on to name the artist. Occasionally, if the person were of particular distinction, there may be more than one portrait referred to. It is therefore with some embarrassment that I have to reveal that in the possession of my family are no fewer than four oil paintings of myself, together with a bust, a drawing and innumerable photographic studies, mostly of me posing rather awkwardly wearing a Guards bearskin and sword. In one I materialised in the photographer's studio with my tunic and bearskin but without my dress trousers; nonetheless the session proceeded and I am recorded for posterity posing in my tunic, but wearing the trousers of my pinstripe suit.

The chances of my securing an entry to the *Dictionary of National Biography* being nil, and my contention that I have no ego, do not square with there being more formal representations of myself than of, say, Sir Alexander Fleming, discoverer of penicillin. In chronological order they are by John Bratby, Bryan Organ, Nicholas Garland, Jemma Phipps, Julian Barrow, Fiore De Henriquez and Springs. The circumstances of the Bratby portrait arose as a result of a letter he wrote to me in 1980 out of the blue. I had some fleeting celebrity at the time and he told me that he made it a practice, instead of waiting for a commission, to initiate the proceedings by writing to temporary celebrities in the likely knowledge that they will not have got around to having their portraits painted and to offer to do this for free, leaving the subject with the option of purchase.

At that time Bratby lived in Rye and was, frankly, obscure. However, I made an appointment and spent an agreeable two hours sitting in his chaotic studio whilst we chatted, and he worked away at the canvas. It was clearly a portrait of me, although me emerging from a car crash with its kaleidoscope of startling colours. Although it was unfinished, I handed over a cheque for £800 and the painting, hanging at the top of the stairs of our house, is the last thing our three sons see before retiring to their respective bedrooms. Bratby himself achieved some minor celebrity as the champion of the so-called Kitchen Sink School of Realism and his work is now in much demand. He died in 1992.

In 1980, forty years ago, I was approaching my fortieth birthday, which I foolishly decided to mark by giving a dinner-dance at Claridge's, every moment of which I loathed. This party moved my friend Ivan Fallon to forecast in his *Telegraph* column that a party on that scale probably signalled the end of the oil boom (it did!) and Taki wrote an amusing column pretending to be observing the evening through the eyes of a waiter.

The only physical survivor of that event is oil painting number two – a portrait by Bryan Organ commissioned by my colleagues on the Board of Cluff Oil. These included my good friends Tommy Pilkington (Chief Steward of the Jockey Club) and Monty Finniston (eminent scientist and Fellow of the Royal

Society). Bryan was I believe at the top of his form at the time, having painted memorable portraits of Harold Macmillan, Prince Charles, and Princess Diana, all of which reside in the National Portrait Gallery.

Bryan, forty-five years old, came on two occasions to my flat in Eaton Square where he took a load of photographs, and was a delightful companion for a couple of hours. He eventually produced a large portrait of me sitting in a chair, legs crossed and wearing a chalk-stripe suit and a rather worried look. At the time I had a few reservations about it, partially because he seemed to have forgotten my neck. In the event I have come to realise that it is a most intelligent and intuitive study, and the anxious look on my face reflected accurately the restlessness of my nature. I now prize it.

Portrait number three is also treasured, in this case a drawing of my wife and me on our wedding day in Hong Kong in September 1993 by Nicholas Garland.

Portrait number four is a three-quarter-length oil painting by Jemma Phipps. By this time I was in my mid-sixties, and this is a conventional study of me standing in my library holding a book. Jemma required a number of sittings in her Chelsea Studio, which were enlivened by her charm and humour, not to mention her beauty. Some years later I had commissioned Julian Barrow to paint the exterior of a London Club, of which I was very fond. Julian had a studio in Tite Street which he shared with Jemma. Tragically Julian died just after finishing my commission. I arranged with Julian's wife for me to go round to the gallery, collect the picture and pay for it. When I arrived, there was Jemma who showed me the handsome small painting.

'But he didn't sign it!' I wailed.

Jemma promptly whipped out a paint brush and inscribed 'Julian Barrow'. So, I have a rare Barrow signed by Barrow aka Jemma Phipps.

The London scene of the early 1980s was graced by a clever and attractive girl – Sarah St George. Her appeal was in no way diminished by cruel injuries she endured as a result of a water-skiing accident in the Bahamas. Brave and beautiful, she was much admired by the male sex although her inclination was and is entirely Sapphic. I was one of the males who failed to breach that barrier but I regularly dined her out and on one of these occasions she advised me that I should have myself sculpted by a friend of hers – Fiore De Henriquez. Fiore was quite something, a hermaphrodite in fact, although since she wore calf-length boots and a huge smock it was quite difficult to determine what she was other than a fully paid-up member of the sisterhood. She had a studio where she held court unless she was at her Italian villa. I duly signed on for a bust and reported for duty half a dozen times at the studio where there was always a middle-aged divorcee in attendance and the conversation was friendly but brittle and challenging. It was with some relief that the final session occurred.

I paid up and carted the excellent product to my office and placed it in the boardroom. Shortly afterwards one of my colleagues, Michael McAllister, confided in me over lunch next door at Pruniers (now alas no more) that if you were looking at a reason to sell shares in a company one of them is unquestionably when the Chief Executive fills the office with busts and portraits of himself. Definitely a sign of an out-of-control ego and a sell signal. I could see the sense in this advice so the next weekend I lugged the thing down to my house in Kent where for a while it shared a cupboard with an even larger bust of Cecil Rhodes, which I had just bought from Barclays Bank in Johannesburg who were too feeble to display it in their boardroom. My bust is now in the hall where it looks handsome and is always adorned by my sons with sunglasses and top hats. Cecil Rhodes, a fine piece by Derwent Wood, I have, against the prevailing anti-colonial trend, removed from the cupboard and it is now prominently displayed on a plinth and elicits no comment from anyone. It is doubtless assumed to be my grandfather! For many years I did have an oil painting of Smuts in the boardroom wearing his Field Marshal's uniform (he was uniquely a member of the War Cabinet in both World Wars). This also elicited no comments even from African politicians until one day an educated Englishman said to me: 'Is that your father?'

'No,' I replied, 'that is Field Marshal Smuts, my father was a Chief Inspector in the Police in the Second World War.'

It was clear that he had never heard of Smuts. I eventually donated the portrait to a charity, The Remembrance Trust, and it was gallantly bought by a neighbour, John May.

John Springs or Springs as he is always known, is a most sympathetic, original and talented artist with a gift for caricatures. He is a Yorkshireman by birth but leavened by a distinctly un-Yorkshire sense of humour and of fun, with the emphasis on understatement and allusion and an encyclopaedic knowledge of what used to be funny in Britain. His centre of gravity is the bar of the Chelsea Arts Club where he can be found when not in his Dovehouse Street Studio. He affects a characteristically individualistic dress style, rather like Whistler minus the monocle. It is his talent for turning something truly ordinary into an excellent running joke which renders him such good company. He executed portrait number four.

So here I sit surrounded by images of myself at varying points in life's journey. Maybe my three sons will find a home for them in their houses eventually and, when their friends say, 'Is that your father?' they can reply, 'Yes! Not a bad old stick!'

16

THE OLD SCHOOL TIE

THE DETERIORATION IN male costume is now virtually complete, with a kind of classless mess the result. This relentless uniformity of life is the source of many of our problems. Everyone wears the same clothes, listens to the same music and so on. You fly from Aberdeen in Scotland to Wellington in New Zealand, as I once did, and find you are confronted by the same brand names you left behind. No wonder people long for some mystery in their lives. The positive outcome of COVID-19 is the decline in flying, which may have a beneficial impact on the environment whilst reviving local customs and characteristics.

The tie, along with the hat and the suit, has now all but evaporated, being given a final shove by COVID-19. Club and Regimental ties were banned by the last Labour Government for magistrates for fear that they could render the defendants 'uncomfortable'. After I read that, I seldom wore anything else. Of course, they are designed to make people uncomfortable because they are not entitled to wear them. The grandest clubs either do not have ties at all (White's, Royal Yacht Squadron) or have ties which are so hideous (MCC and the Garrick Club) that you really would not want to wear them even if you were a member, although at Lord's one occasionally sees in the pavilion members wearing MCC hats, ties, jackets and socks!

The two most elegant ties are the regimental ones – the Guards (red and blue) and the Rifle Brigade. I was admonished once by my friend Tim Tollemache, Lord Lieutenant of Suffolk, and a stickler, for wearing my brigade tie upside down, which I did not think was possible. This was at the Memorial Service for our friend Patrick Lichfield at the Guards' Chapel. Patrick only had one tie – the brigade tie of which he was very proud.

Similarly, I alternate between wearing a brigade tie and, in London, a white tie with a black suit and a white shirt. This makes me look like a cross between a property developer and a head waiter, but it is my 'signature', as they say in those idiotic colour supplement profiles.

I recall when I was in my twenties in London many of the older club men still wore waisted jackets, carnations, monocles, and spats. You would be a brave man to walk down Piccadilly dressed like that today.

I think the height of male fashion was represented by the frock coat which, complemented by a glittering top hat and white spats, has never been surpassed. That was an Edwardian phenomenon, and come to think of it that's the age in which I should have lived. The problem today lies in the cost of being well dressed – a suit by a first-class tailor such as Edward Sexton is five thousand pounds. Too much. But instead of compromising and buying a cheaper suit, most people dress 'casually' in this country. Alas, whereas Italian, Spanish and French males look elegant in casual attire the British look like tramps … and of course behave like them.

17

Lord Williams of Elvel

I N 1972 I was riding high. I had realised that
the UK's North Sea was set to become one
of the world's most prolific oil-producing
basins and, notwithstanding the fact that I
had only recently left the Army as a youthful
Captain, I contrived to become a part of the
North Sea oil fraternity by pressuring trusting
friends to put up £300,000 (£3 million equiv-
alent now) to fund an application for various
licences and I had further managed to persuade
the Ministry of Fuel and Power (as it then was)
to award us them. Quite how I managed this
is of some interest, but it came down to the
senior civil servant (Angus Beckett) having the
courage and confidence to see his duty as not
only striving to get the North Sea explored as
rapidly as possible, but also as creating some
new British oil companies in the process, as I
have described in *Get On With It* (2016).

From the moment that I read in the *Financial*

Times that the Government was about to invite offers (in work not cash) for four hundred North Sea oil blocks I resolved to join in the fray. Since I had left the Army I had stood for Parliament (unsuccessfully) and worked for an imaginative new merchant bank, the Ionian. The Ionian, under the leadership of the flamboyant Michael Behrens, had had the imagination also to perceive the North Sea's potential and formed Oil Exploration Holdings as a vehicle, ably run by the present Lord Esher, a languid and intelligent individual. He is the son of Lionel Brett, the architect, whose appointment as President of the Royal Institute of British Architects coincided with a great storm blowing all the roofs off the houses in one of the so-called 'New Towns' that he had designed! He also apparently presided at a meeting of the RIBA when on the agenda was an item – inserted by Brett himself – to consider the most suitable method of celebrating the 100th anniversary of the birth of the controversial Sir Basil Spence. There was a long silence before someone said: 'Why don't we blow one of his buildings up?'

So, I pondered how, as a complete unknown, I might set about this task. Other than BP and the Anglo-Dutch Shell Company and Burmah Oil (about to go bust), there really were no

British Oil companies (with one or two distinguished small exceptions: Carless, really a
service company, Trinidad Canadian, Ultramar
and Premier). The expertise and the financial
resources were largely North American. As it
happened, when I was supinely representing the
Ionian Bank in New York I had met, socially,
Chris Dohm, a tough ex-Amoco Executive,
who had, as was and is common practice in
North America, founded his own oil company
– Transworld Petroleum. I quickly realised
that there was a certain symmetry between the
names of these companies and their worth: the
grander the name the smaller the company! In
any event I persuaded Dohm and his charming
ex-Amoco partner John Tolleson to join with
me in a joint venture to submit an application
for two North Sea blocks 21/1 and 21/6. Our
consortium was composed of 70% Transworld
Petroleum and 30% my collection of stalwart
friends. Together with one small corporate,
Charterhall, and our own geologist, Fred
Stugard, who consulted under the corporate
identity of Petromin, the consortium company
accordingly was identified as CCP North Sea
Associates (Cluff, Charterhall and Petromin).

I have related before in *Get On With It* the
adventures we had in obtaining the licences but

following the euphoria of receiving the awards we were faced with the prospect of finding our share of the money required to drill the first exploration well. However, by chance I was introduced to the investment bank Barings and the partner who was selected to advise and guide CCP was, curiously, C. C. P. Williams. His 'CCP' stood for Charles Cuthbert Powell. He was primarily chosen to advise us because he had worked for BP for six years from 1958 to 1964 after Christ Church and the London School of Economics.

I quickly realised that Charles was an unusual individual – exceptionally intelligent and apparently rather a cold fish, although I soon detected that he had a sense of humour, concealed by his shyness. Along with Peter Cooper, the Chairman of CCP and an experienced stock broker, we raised CCP's contribution to the drilling of our first well 21/1-1 which was the discovery well of what became the Buchan Field. Shortly afterwards it became evident that Charles, a committed Christian Socialist, was not comfortable working for Barings and it was no surprise when he left to chair the Price Commission in 1977. Eventually he became the leader of the Labour Party in the House of Lords as Lord Williams of Elvel.

From 1993 he developed a parallel life as an author, with acclaimed biographies of de Gaulle, Adenauer, Petain and Macmillan. Another dimension to his life was the game of cricket. He had played for Oxford and Essex and produced an intelligent biography of Bradman.

In 1975 he had married Jane Portal, whom I had got to know by reason of my membership of the dining club The Other Club, for which she was for many years the Secretary, having previously been one of Winston Churchill's assistants. In fact, she is the sole survivor of that dedicated and long-suffering team. Previously married, she also had a son with Anthony Montague; that son, it has been recently revealed, is Justin Welby, the present Archbishop of Canterbury, who by a curious coincidence was an accountant working in the North Sea oil business whilst Charles and I were scheming to fund CCP North Sea Associates.

I often wonder whether, had Charles Williams not joined the Labour Party and chaired the Price Commission, but had remained at Barings, that bank would not have collapsed. It was a monumental failure of control which finished Barings off, but poor management had evolved into a culture which

I do not believe Charles would have tolerated, had he been en poste in the early 1980s. I do not think I have, other than the assassination of President Kennedy, experienced a greater shock than when I read in the *Sunday Telegraph* that Barings was insolvent. I recall being told by Christopher Heath, who had previously run Barings' Far East business before being axed, that had he not been fired the Singapore office would not have brought the Bank down simply because whenever the Singapore office received a large order he would call the Bank of America or whoever had instigated it and thank them. Since these orders had been forged by Leeson, the Singapore trader, the answer would have come: 'What order?' and Leeson's duplicity would have been quickly ascertained. So, I present two hypotheses: firstly, would Barings have survived had Charles Williams remained there; and secondly would the crisis have occurred at all had Christopher Heath not been fired? I should add that I have discussed this with various Barings executives, many of whom went on to have distinguished further careers, and in particular with John Bolsover, all of whom remain loyal to Peter Baring.

This chapter is really a tribute to Charles Williams, a most distinguished member of his generation, who were it not for his modesty, would have been very much more of a public figure.

18

ADRIAN DAINTREY

I N JUNE 1973 I was introduced to Adrian
Daintrey, as I had let it be known that I
wanted a series of watercolours done of my
beloved cliff top house. We first met at lunch
at the Chelsea Arts Club of which he was a
member, although I picked up the bill. This was
the first rule of Daintrey's Law – never pay! This
was of no consequence to me as I was infected
by Adrian's rather louche charm. The first bottle
was seen off whilst Adrian explained that he
had fallen hopelessly in love with the Jamaican
conductress on whatever bus it was that bore
him up and down the King's Road. During the
second bottle we scratched out on the menu a
sort of contract which I recall simply stated that
I would be responsible for his board and lodg-
ing during the time it took him to complete his
task. Being rather the worse for wear after the
second bottle, together with a large Armagnac,
I omitted to determine how long he estimated

it would take to complete one watercolour and subsequently my wine merchant was preparing for an early retirement when I settled Adrian's malt whisky bill. However, I was well pleased with the result, which hangs in my study as I write. He also went on to produce a charming study for me of Mr Kent who for many years presided over Carlin's cigar shop in Park Place, on the ground floor of the rickety building where in those days I had my first London office. Every morning I used to collect my daily cigar from Mr Kent and sit on a leather upright chair 'shooting the breeze' with Mr Kent and his even older assistant. I have that picture in my kitchen in London and salute it every morning, as I have done since 1974. Alas, Carlins ceased trading on Mr Kent's retirement. I never knew what his Christian name was.

Adrian went on producing records of my favourite places: the second hole at Royal St George's Golf Club, the entrance to the Guards Club then in Charles Street, the house I owned in the south of France, all of which I still have.

Anthony Powell in his three-volume journals describes Adrian as being his 'oldest' friend. As a Carthusian it was with some symmetry that he was allowed to end his days in the Charterhouse, a charitable cloistered retreat for ailing gentlefolk in the City of London. There, still tended by a brood of loyal girl friends, including the glamorous and gifted Candia McWilliam, he slowly withdrew.

Adrian's liver gave up in 1988 after a lunch-time binge and I was sad to say farewell to him and to those happy dinners at L'Etoile in Charlotte Street and the White Tower in Percy Street. Recently, to my surprise, I came across my name in Anthony Powell's diaries where he records a discussion of who should give the address at Adrian's funeral. Names were apparently proposed, including 'a tycoon named Algy Cluff previously unknown to me', he remarks witheringly! As recorded by Powell, he 'left his body for dissection' which 'should make medical history'.

During the Charterhouse period he was taken up by Sally Hunter Fine Art and he enjoyed a late flurry of celebrity. As I have said I collected Adrian's oils and watercolours. He had been stationed in Cairo during the war as a most unwilling private in the camouflage section. Whilst there he executed a number of oil paintings, for one of which – the interior of Shepheard's Hotel – I paid £2,500 in 1979. I had a friend, an Arabist Tory MP, who much admired it, and so when he married for the third time I gave him my Daintrey of Cairo as a wedding present.

A few years elapsed and my friend, having divorced his third wife, approached me and revealed that he was short of funds, no doubt due to marital exertions. I had always regretted giving him the painting, so I bought it back off him for £800. Somehow, he subsequently discovered that I had originally paid £2,500 for it and he had the nerve to accuse me of deceiving him by not paying £2,500. So feebly I paid him another £1,700. I therefore paid the world-record price for a Daintrey twice! Worse, it has subsequently disappeared.

Should it ever resurface I shall decline the offer of buying it a third time.

19

Two Forgotten Books

URING A LONG and active life there has been one constant – books. From the age of eight I have read virtually every day, barring enforced military solitude in the Borneo jungle in 1965. Otherwise, without fail I would read or reread at least one book, although often I have as many as four open in tandem – most likely a Wodehouse, the letters or diaries of Evelyn Waugh, a military biography and a mid-twentieth-century crime novel.

As I began to travel widely in the Far East and Africa, I always visited local bookshops, be they in Singapore, Hong Kong, Johannesburg or Cape Town. After a while I became a dedicated collector of Africana in particular, but also biography and anything relating to Borneo, Malaya and Hong Kong as well as commercial histories of oil, mining, shipping and trading companies. Many dealers became good friends, especially Michael Brand, the scholarly and unpompous proprietor of Marlborough Rare Books. Others included Robin Fryde who ran Thorolds Bookshop in Harrison Street in the Central Business District of Johannesburg for fifty years. He had trained as a lawyer and had bought legal books from Frank Thorold, the founder, and subsequently took over the business. It was a magnificent, unruly shop, with books and paintings from floor to ceiling, with Robin himself a most enchanting and knowledgeable individual, always number one on the list of people to visit when in South Africa on business. He helped Harry Oppenheimer build his collection, housed at his famous Johannesburg house Brenthurst, and he helped me with my Africana library, most of which came from him.

Robin had been involved in a most unusual lawsuit concerning the sale of a book from the collection of Sir Alfred Beit. Beit was the nephew of Alfred Beit, the founder of the firm of Wernher, Beit & Co., diamond dealers, and the son of Sir Otto Beit, the First Baronet. Sir Alfred died childless, having spent his life as close to his money as possible, and correspondingly as far away from the Inland Revenue as possible. This involved living in Ireland where he and his wife, Clementine, were mugged and burgled by an IRA gang, led rather incongruously by an upper middle class English lady, Rose Dugdale. In 1991 Sir Alfred's copy of Le Vaillant's *Voyage to the Interior of Africa* appeared in an auction in Cape Town. The bidding was between Clarke's Bookshop in Cape Town and Thorolds, and rapidly increased from R40k to R80k. Robin claimed, as reported by Sheila Markham in the trade press, that the book was knocked down to him at R80k, and the final bid had been called eleven times by the auctioneer. Suddenly a private collector in the front row (Robin was in the back row) said 'I bid', and the Auctioneer reopened the bidding by calling R85k. The bidding accelerated to R300k with Robin continuing to bid to 'protect his interest'. He then tendered R80k in payment, which was refused and Sir Alfred Beit's estate sued the Auctioneers for R300k.

About four years ago I was appointed as custodian of the Royal Yacht Squadron's remarkable library, which has added another and welcome dimension to my book collecting, albeit on behalf of the Squadron. I have been ably assisted by Gwyneth Mitchell the assistant librarian, and together we have strived to maintain the library's preeminent position amongst private marine collections. Thanks to the indefatigable

Commodore David Hughes the entire library is now accessible online. Another dealer I have had the pleasure of being advised by is Adrian Harrington, past President of the Antiquarian Booksellers Association, from whom I have learnt a lot. Together we have reorganised the library and made some judicious purchases.

***

In this final chapter I refer to two books which have given me much pleasure, but both of which are forgotten, and I quote from them in the hope of arousing some interest amongst my readership. This chapter is not directed – heaven forbid – at the scholar but at my fellow bibliophiles and is modelled on my favourite anthology: *Have You Anything to Declare?* by Maurice Baring. I have found much solace in that treasury and indeed used a quotation found within on the headstone of my parents' grave: 'Something strong and genial and immeasurably kind has gone out of the world leaving it too much the poorer for thought to endure.' – Alexander Laing. Baring compiled *Have You Anything to Declare?* at his house in Rottingdean and it was published in 1936. He declares that it is a list not an anthology and there is no theme to it, just a random series of quotations. Some come with learned commentary, others left to stand alone. In that time of plenty, many pages display one line only, but that single line invariably holds my attention for as long as if it had been a whole page.

Baring was born in 1874 and died in Scotland in 1945 of paralysis agitans, being looked after at Beaufort Castle, Beauly, Inverness-shire by the Lovat family. During his life he had been a diplomat, a journalist, an author, and an officer in the Royal Flying Corps. *Have You Anything to Declare?* was to be his last book. His immense culture renders the book a delightful companion to be constantly revisited.

I quote the following extracts:

'We do not know which was Sappho's last poem, but there is no sadder poem than the single line:
"I loved thee once, Atthis, long ago."'

And from Webster's *The Duchess of Malfi*:
'Why should only I, Of all the other princes of the world, Be cas'd up, like a holy relic? I have youth, And a little beauty.'

From *Don Quixote*:
'And she is as tall as a lance, as fresh as an April Morning, and as strong as a porter.'

From *Isaiah*:
'Thine eyes shall see the king in his beauty: they shall behold the land of far distances.'

Wordsworth:
'About the fields I wander, knowing this Only, that what I seek I cannot find.'

This anthology, I see from my inscription, dated '22/1/1994 Harare', was purchased from a bookshop in the Borrowdale shopping centre, which was run by Mrs Graham, the mother of my then exploration director in Zimbabwe, Nicholas Graham. I had a house at 16 Orange Grove Drive, opposite the Forestry Commission (where my wife and I planted two mahogany trees in the garden to honour the birth of two of our sons, Harry and Philip. I expect they remain there thirty years later). The reason for my visit was a tragic one – it was to attend the funeral of the Minister of Mines, Christopher Ushewokunze, who had been killed in mysterious circumstances in a car crash, a method favoured by Mugabe's special police force.

Journey to Java
by Harold Nicolson

On Harold Nicolson's seventieth birthday on 21 November 1956 he received an 'enormous' cheque from two hundred and fifty friends, which he elected to spend on a journey from England to Java with his wife on the Rotterdam Lloyd Line's MV *Willem Ruys*. They left on 15 January 1957 and returned on 21 March and Nicolson describes the voyage as being 'two of the happiest months I have ever enjoyed'. I have three copies of this enchanting book, the first bought when I was eighteen in 1958. It is probably the least known among his oeuvre, and indeed his grandson told me that he has never read it, but it is an entirely satisfactory companion to be reopened and reread at any page and at any time. I make no apology for the lengthy extracts which I have selected.

He sets himself the task of compiling a diary of life on board ship, which is of historical interest, and he writes amusingly and shrewdly of his fellow passengers, but this is the packaging as it were of a volume with a serious purpose, being an inquiry into the nature of causeless melancholy. He has brought on board a small library including works by Galen, Rousseau,

Burton, Novalis and skilfully combines his serious purpose with entertaining vignettes and reports of the progress of the *Willem Ruys*. Here the ship is off Dakar:

> I wake up at 4.30 a.m. and look out of my casement. I see a lighthouse winking patiently and below and around it a tiny coruscation of lights quivering. It is Dakar. I get up, put on a dressing-gown, cross the passage and rouse V. It is not, I know, really worth it, but I hate seeing anything of the slightest interest without sharing it with her. She will be interested to observe the African continent, which until now has kept away from us, could swing or bulge so suddenly and so close that we can see lights at four in the morning twinkling beside a tower. To me those lights recall de Gaulle and the agony of his failure to capture Dakar and French Africa. We were told at the time that some of his staff had spoken indiscreetly of the coming venture and that the Vichy Government had thus been warned in advance and had been given time to prepare their resistance. Only a man of de Gaulle's superhuman faith, resolution and self-confidence could have survived such a fiasco. As it was, the utter failure of his expedition embittered the already taut personal

relationship between him and Churchill and confirmed our General Staff in their suspicion that the Free French represented a security risk. Thus in the future our plans were concealed from them, and de Gaulle was deeply hurt by our unwillingness to keep him fully informed in advance of such operations as the North African and Normandy landings, with which he claimed with some justice that he was intimately concerned. Curious that a little nest of lights sparkling across dark waters should recall to me so vividly the picture of this tall man trembling with suppressed rage in his study at Carlton Gardens. I sympathized with his mortification, I profoundly admired his courage, and kneeling there on my bunk watching the lights of Dakar swing past us I exclaimed 'Vive de Gaulle! Vive de Gaulle!' then I pulled up my little shutter again and went to sleep.

Then he dilates on time.

It is interesting to observe how insistent, even when one has transformed the external circumstances of life, is the force of habit. I have already noted in this diary how often I have been startled by the realization that, when both time and space are regulated by forces utterly beyond one's own control, it ceases to concern one whether one is in Lat. 38° or Lat. N.04°, whether today is tomorrow, or whether it be 11.55 in the morning or 3.24 in the afternoon. This liberation from engagements and appointments has shown me how, in my English routine, I am at the mercy of a time-table. I had hitherto assumed that my days were more or less my own and unregulated by anything but my own whims or volition. I was called at 8.0, had my breakfast at 8.30, read the newspaper, dictated my letters, wrote a review or an article during the morning, went out to luncheon, attended some committee or visited some gallery or flower show in the afternoon, read a book during the evening, had some friends to visit me, had my bath and changed, dined somewhere, and eventually retired to bed, wholly unaware that throughout the day I had been disciplined and harassed. On Fridays, by the 3.15 from Charing Cross, I would go down to Sissinghurst, work during the mornings, do some light gardening in the afternoon, read books all evening, and perhaps look at television for half an hour or so after dinner.

I now realise that always I was being bullied by the clock on the mantelpiece (I am not among those who say 'chimneypiece' when they mean mantelpiece) and that my engagement had become a despot ordering me to do this or to do that and to be up and about. My engagement book, as I have said, now lies idly in a drawer of the dressing table and no telephone can shrill. There is no reason at all why I should not allow the hours to drift by me, sitting in the sunshine looking for flying fish, or discussing with my fellow passengers whether it is profitable or the reverse to nip off the minor shoots of the delphinium in the month of May.

Yet such is the force of the habit that I have evolved myself a marine time-table for the purpose of this voyage. Being a romantic, V. regards this reversion to the automatic with contempt. I explain to her that if one is by nature orderly one cannot slough this disposition merely because one has crossed the Equator. Moreover, I believe that the human brain is largely mechanical in its functioning, that it requires a certain regular rhythm, and that a time-table is a fly-wheel which sets the whole apparatus on the swing. 'Nonsense!' she answers, 'you are sacrificing the whole benefit of the journey owing to an illusion which you acquired when you were a civil servant. You are incapable of leisure.' I have noticed, however, that she also spends the whole morning and the whole afternoon working in her cabin at *La Grande Mademoiselle*: but I do not say so. I merely elaborate my own time-table with greater detail and in greater precision. Obstinacy is among the more unexpected components of the bourgeois mind.

...

V. thinks that, did I possess greater willpower, I should take this opportunity to waste my time.

As an antidote to causeless melancholy there is a touching reference to causeless exhilaration.

The table next to ours in the dining saloon is occupied by English people, forming a covey of young married couples going out to the Far East. There are Doctor O'Malley and his wife; he is a young Irish surgeon of splendid appearance who has got an appointment in Malaya. There are Mr and Mrs Emmett. He has an air of a Bloomsbury intellectual and I derive the mistaken impression that he is going out as an inspector of British Council schools and institutes in Southeast Asia. I discover later that in fact he is one of the world's leading experts upon the planting and marketing of tea. Mrs Emmett is a vivacious and engaging young woman who wears a different frock every evening; she must have been told when a girl that she possessed a musical laugh, since her gusts of merriment are frequent and prolonged. She is, I suspect, an example of causeless exhilaration, and as such does not come within the scope of my particular enquiry. There are two or three other young people at their table and their laughter echoes continuously upon the ceiling of the saloon. At dinner this evening they are ominously hushed and when we come upstairs later, we are told that all dances and entertainments have been cancelled. It seems that this morning, when we were gazing at Mauritius, a flying officer travelling second class with his wife and child to Singapore fell overboard. It took his distraught wife some three hours before she was certain that he had disappeared before she told the captain. We were by then some hundred miles from the scene of the misfortune and there was nothing that the Captain de Jonge could do beyond sending a wireless to the Governor of Mauritius and warning the R.A.F at Colombo. We are sobered by this occurrence; the orchestra refrains from playing 'Que serà serà' and the great ship plunges imperviously onward through the night.

An example of his interest in his fellow passengers:

I am sitting reading on deck when a man comes and sits beside me, saying, 'I hope I do not interrupt.' It is the melancholy Clitheroe, whose name, I have since discovered, is not Clitheroe at all, but Sidney Culpeper, a descendant I assume of the astrologist and herbalist, and of all the other Culpepers who lie buried in Goudhurst tombs. 'May I ask,' he continues with dry politeness, 'what it is you are reading with such absorption?' 'I am reading *Obermann*,' I answer. At this he sighs deeply. 'Ah yes,' he sighs, 'Matthew Arnold's friend.' Then without a word he gets up and walks away. I must talk to him again.

At Singapore:

We were glad to meet our friend Boumphrey in the saloon. He had come on board to revisit the *Willem Ruys* and to greet his former fellow passengers before they returned home. He had brought with him a little Chinese clue and white bowl which he presented to V. He told us that his wife's ankle had not mended itself and that she was now in hospital and might have to have an operation. We were sorry about this. A messenger arrived bearing an enormous bunch of orchids for V. which had been picked for her by Lady Scott, the wife of the Commissioner General. We were touched by this act of courtesy. The Stedalls have rejoined the boat having spent a week at Kuala Lumpur. Their daughter and son-in-law had come down to see them off and I regret that two such attractive people should not be coming back with us to Southampton. Mrs Stedall tells me that her daughter, in expectation of their visit, had planted a moon flower in her garden arousing curiosity and pleasure. Then we go down to our cabins, and V. arranges Lady Scott's orchids in the pots she bought at Bandung. I do not eat much dinner, since the soup at the Peking Restaurant has made me feel sick inside. I, who used to be able to eat anything without the slightest reaction! Such are the penalties of old age.

Page 164

It was Epicurus who taught us that only by natural philosophy could man master his fear of life and death. The gods, even if they exist, are utterly indifferent to human suffering; the sequence of seasons, the majestic rhythm of the stars, are not due to divine ordering but to natural causes; pleasure, or the avoidance of pain and fear, is the true guide to life – '*dux vitae dia voluptas*': the wiseman will not sadden himself, by nurturing unattainable desires; he will imitate the gods, who live in quietude, 'smiling secretly'. Above all, he will not allow his tranquillity to be disturbed by superstitious nonsense regarding future penalties or rewards; when a man dies, he becomes non-existent and therefore death should mean nothing more to him than a dreamless sleep. This splendid quietude can be achieved by a study of natural philosophy, by belief in the atoms 'ruining along the illimitable inane', and by the exercise of reason. Fear was an inevitable affliction for the superstitious man. 'Through every wood,' he writes, 'throughout the vast mountains and the deep forests, terror creeps with shaking limbs.' The superior man can be liberated from guilt and fear. 'The faults', he writes, 'that reason is unable to subjugate are so trivial that nothing should prevent us from living a life of tranquillity like that of the immortal gods.'

Yet Lucretius, in spite of his persistent wish to rid himself and others from the oppressions of guilt and fear, was not wholly an escapist.

He contended that a man should make the best of his own opportunities for productive living – '*vitaque mancipio nulli datur: omnibus usu.*' A magnificently unhappy man was Lucretius and his fierce poetry should render us ashamed of our contentment. But how wonderful it is to communicate again with the vigour of such conviction and to allow his mighty line to linger in the ear, while seated on the deck of M. V. *Willem Ruys*, gazing out on the angry sea, *turbantibus aequora ventis.*

Page 179

But I come back to Epictetus, who was in truth a charming and extremely witty person. He taught that if a man desired contentment he must 'make the best of his own faculties and take everything else as it happens to occur'. What really matters is not what we do but the way in which we do it. 'We should be careful', he said, 'how we play the game, but utterly indifferent to the ball itself.' If we are to avoid anxieties and disappointments, or what dear Mrs Carter calls 'solicitude', then we must concentrate on internals, which are within the control of our own will and reason and ignore externals which are outside our control. What

I like about Epictetus is that he disbelieved in pessimism and regarded the 'ivory tower' school as something that was contrary to nature. 'You were not born', he told his pupils, 'to be depressed and unhappy in society; you were born to enjoy yourselves in the company of your fellows.' 'Solitude', he said, 'is the state of a helpless person'; and he contended that a man who shirked all social responsibilities could never develop the valuable virtues of fidelity and honour. Although himself an extremely austere man he disapproved of the squalor practised by the cynics as by some subsequent ascetics. He insisted that his pupils should blow their noses properly, wash with soap and water, and clean their teeth. His *Enchiridion* or manual is replete with shrewd worldly aphorisms, devised for the avoidance of displeasure. It is a mistake to be fussy when one goes to the public baths, or irritated when the maid upsets the oil-can, or concerned with the seat you are allotted at dinner party, or to laugh too loud, or to listen to authors reading their own works, or to show off in front of less educated people, or to be self-satisfied. 'If you really want to be good', he said, 'you must begin by convincing yourself that you are bad.' 'Grasshoppers are musical', he said, 'but snails are dumb.' 'Remember', he said, 'that you are an actor in a drama and that it is the author who decides how it will end.' 'You will prove unconquerable', he said – and this in fact was the essence of his teaching – 'if you enter into no contest which you are unlikely to win.'

I admit that such precepts are shrewd rather than noble. I do not like the Stoics much more than I like the Epicureans; but I like Epictetus of Prevesa or Nicopolis much more than I like Epicurus of Samos and Mitylene.

Pages 204–206

I wait for her in the smoking room and have just started opening letters when Peter Lycett Green appears. He has forgiven us for having, in momentary confusion, chucked him on our previous visit and has come to take us round and give us luncheon at Morgenster. He has been suffering from asthma and does not look well, but then asthmatic people vary in their appearance from hour to hour. I give him an orange juice which is all the drink one can obtain when in harbour and we sit there talking about life and letters until V. returns. Then at about 11.0 we at last disembark and enter Peter's car, which contains a poodle and Mr Burnham.

He takes us straight to Kirstenbosch, not to the main gardens which we had seen before, but to the adjoining nursery. We find it most interesting. He shows us the frames where, in little pans, they cultivate and propagate the fantastic vegetation of the Karroo desert. They are the strangest little plants that I have ever seen. At first sight they look like a group of fourteen or fifteen different-sized pebbles mainly of a brown or dull grey colour. On closer inspection one sees that they are in fact growing plants, capable of expansion and division, and some of them bearing tiny little scabs on their surface which are no mere abrasions but organs of generations.

We then drive on to Groot Constantia. It stands in an amphitheatre of precipices and blue mountains, surrounded by vineyards and with a view across the Cape Flats below it to the line of the Hottentot mountains. It is approached through an avenue of gnarled oaks. Groot Constantia formed part of the estate acquired in the seventeenth century by Simon van der Stel. It included such other farm-houses as Klein Constantia, Hoop op Constantia, Witte Boomen and Buitenverwachting, which is the Dutch for 'Beyond all expectation'. The present house was built by Hendrik Cloete in 1790, the architect being Louis Michel Thibault, pupil of Gabriel, and the plaster-work and decoration being executed by the German, Anton Anreith. The house was destroyed by fire in 1925 but reconstructed from the original designs and arranged and furnished as a national museum, one passes under the great white gable by a carved teak front door, above which is a niche and statue, into cool dark rooms, floored with Batavian tiles, roofed with neat beams, and containing specimens of Cape Dutch furniture and a few pictures. The stoep outside gives on to a terrace from which one descends by a few steps to a small garden. In the centre there is a placid pool enlivened by a single blue water-lily standing pertly erect from its flat leaves. Beyond this is the wine-store, a long white building with plaster carvings of urchins and grapes above the doorway and inside vast vats of highly polished wood and brass. All the buildings are whitewashed, but as the surface of the walls are uneven the bright sun does not strike uniformly, but with all manner of shades and undertones. The roods are thatched with the South African reed, which is unlike our straw thatching at home, since it is smooth and gives the impression of a moleskin cloth. As an example of simplicity, suitability and elegance

I should place Groot Constantia among the masterpieces of domestic architecture. Had the town-planners of Cape Town developed the Dutch theme they could have created one of the most beautiful cities on this earth in place of the Victorian and Detroit jumble that now disfigures the site. V. and I again become angry at such lack of intelligence and taste. We then drive to Morgenster which is Peter's own house. It also is in the Cape Dutch style, with a fine gable enriched with baroque plaster work, a stoep, and a library, drawing room and dining room, in which his furniture, books and pictures look fine indeed. He shows us his garden. It is a gardener's garden, displaying specimen plants and trees in little beds surrounded by stone copings. It is the wrong time of the year, corresponding to our English August, and but few of these precious plants were still in flower. But V. enjoyed it all immensely, since like most professional gardeners she derives ecstasy from reading the labels. We then have an excellent luncheon and are given Nederburg 1954, as good a white wine as I have tasted since I lived in Germany.

Peter drives us back to Cape Town and we stop at a shop which sells curios and other souvenirs designed for tourists. It contains Zulu shields, assegais and knobkerries; views of Table Mountain painted upon slabs of local wood; lion's claws made into neat little brooches; and a variety of bags and belts constructed of Zebra hides, and the skins of pythons and other reptiles. I am assailed by boatfuss and V. with her usual unselfishness tears herself away from these delights, although unwillingly. We drive back to the dock, say goodbye to Peter, and clamber on board at 3.15.

We read our letters. As usual there are long, vivid, detailed and amusing letters from Ben and Nigel. Few men as busy as they are would take the trouble to write their travelling parents at such length. We are grateful. Nigel says that the Chairman and the local Committee in Bournemouth East have refused to admit any new members to the Conservative Association, fearing that many of those who wish to retain Nigel as their sitting Member might outvote the Caucus. I doubt whether they are legally entitled to establish a closed shop in this way. In any case their action is unfair, and indicates that, not being sure of the justice of their attitude, they are determined to adopt totalitarian methods, I am disgusted and sad.

We cast off at 5.0. 'There you see', comments V., 'I told you there were heaps of time and we could easily have stayed another hour at that nice stop.' It is not that she really cherishes a love for assegais or lion-claw brooches, but that she likes collecting her numerous Christmas presents well in advance and assumes that the simple recipients will welcome such outlandish objects. We watch the parapets of South Africa receding in the evening sun, it is cold and I wear my ordinary dinner jacket and not my white dinner jacket in the evening. Again, we put the clock back an hour which for me is always a small despair.

Pages 207–209

I spend the day reading, for the second time, *The Unquiet Grave* by Palinurus. I am aware that Cyril Connolly, when he wrote it, was in a melancholy mood. He was saddened by the war, obsessed by the invasion and occupation of France, and distraught by personal trouble. It was the memory of one of Virgil's loveliest hexameters that gave to the book both its title and its pseudonym. Yet it depresses me that this beautiful study should, as *The Waste Land*, have exercised so debilitating an effect upon the wills of the young.

I remember that two or three years ago I went

down to King's School, Canterbury, to give a talk to their sixth form. When my lecture was over, I was shown the way to the station by one of the prefects, an intelligent youth, who had recently obtained a scholarship at Oxford. The great Cathedral loomed behind us and in front red and white and green, were the lights of British Railways. He told me as we passed through the town that the elder boys really enjoyed it when men of letters came down from London and gave them lectures. 'It takes us', he said, 'out of ourselves'. I was pleased by this and asked him who, among living writers, he would most wish to hear. 'Mr Cyril Connolly,' he answered. I did not suggest to him that of all authors whom I knew Cyril Connolly was the one least calculated to 'take' young people 'out of themselves'. I promised to approach the pundit and, in so far as I recollect, he was invited and went.

Unlike myself, Cyril Connolly, is burdened with a sense of original sin. 'Those of us', he writes, 'who have been brought up as Christians and have lost our faith have retained our sense of sin without the saving belief in redemption.' What is so depressing about him is that he believes the sense of sin to be a good thing and not a bad thing. He calls it 'the taproot of the unconscious' and contends that Goethe and Voltaire are the only two first-class writers who never possessed it. I could think of others, but the point is well made.

I have noticed that those who believe in original sin tend, not only to deplore the evil of this earth, but also to love and cherish guilt-feelings within themselves. It has always puzzled me why Cyril Connolly, who has afforded so much pleasure and given so much opportunity to younger writers, should nurture a load of guilt. True it is that on one occasion he filched three avocado pears from Willy Maugham's garden at Cap Ferrat, but this is not an episode that should weigh upon the conscience of a humanist. Yet he can write of 'the accumulation of guilt and remorse which, like a garbage-can, I carry through life'. I cannot believe that a man of his gifts and vivacity, educated at Eton and Balliol, can, except in moments of ill-health, feel any profound remorse for having dawdled in cafés in Paris or stayed in bed too long playing with lemurs. Such people, conscious of their own talents, are always on the verge of a masterpiece and suffer much from the intuition that their masterpieces, such as *The Unquiet Grave* or the journal *Intime*, may prove to be confessions of their own lack of willpower. It is not something that is due to external circumstance, since Connolly may be confident of writing an even greater work before he dies; it is a matter of internal humours and secretions.

Such accidie is in any case deplorable since it brings with it subsidiary distrusts and disappointments and weakens courage. Thus Connolly, like Baudelaire, is unable to contemplate himself without dismay. He sees himself as 'a fat, slothful, querulous, greedy, impotent carcase', which is a most self-conscious thing to see. He is often visited by what he calls *Angst*, meaning thereby Kierkegaard's dread; namely a sullen combination of ennui, remorse, and anxiety. 'Ennui', he writes, 'is a condition of not fulfilling our potentialities; remorse of not having fulfilled them; and anxiety of not being able to fulfil them.' What is so terrible about *Angst*, he tells us, is that it generates hatred, which is 'crystallised fear'. This is a suggestive comment. Does it explain why the nineteenth century malcontents are indignant? This is a question which, as Mr Colin Wilson would say, must be examined in a subsequent chapter. Yet how strongly does Cyril Connolly remind me of Coleridge. To him also *Angst* was based on a sense of guilt arising from his own indolence and procrastination:

'And fears self-will'd, that shunn'd
   the eyes of hope,
And hope that scarce would know itself
   from fear;
Sense of past youth, and manhood come
   in vain,
And genius given and knowledge won in
   vain,'

Yet Connolly is no irredeemable pessimist. He regards escapist philosophies, even the teaching of the Buddha, as 'a desperate stratagem of failure, the failure of men to be men.' He believes that the pursuit of happiness must never be abandoned and regrets that we have lost the old Delphic formula which taught men that happiness could be found in the insistent practice of temperance and self-knowledge. 'These are now', he writes, but not despairingly, 'beyond the reach of ordinary people, who, owing to the pursuit of violent sensation, can no longer distinguish between pleasure and pain.' He leaves us with the discouraging apophthegm that 'nothing can be accomplished without fanaticism and without serenity nothing can be enjoyed.'
  'Nudus', I fear, 'in ignota, Palinure,
jacebis arena.'

It is rough, with a following wind blowing up from the Antarctic. The two albatross, as Stedall predicted, have left us and turned round to their colder latitudes. The wind of our passage and the wind booming along behind us cancel each other out so exactly that I am able to light a match on deck. I do not bathe as it is too cold, but in the afternoon, it clears up and the wares splash and sparkle in the sun.

Page 250

We reach Waterloo exactly at 2.0 p.m. and are met by Copper, the car, a bewildered Rollo on his lead, and Colin, whose auburn head towers above the other passengers. We stop for a moment at the Albany, where we have some coffee and sandwiches, and then through familiar wet roads drove down to Sissinghurst. We get home at 5.10 while it is still light enough to see that the orchard is ablaze with daffodils.

Thus, ends our Journey to Java, the happiest journey that even we have known.

So also ends the literary journey which I have made many times thanks to the discerning pen of Sir Harold. There obtains a certain similarity with Maurice Baring – now forgotten men of letters who both served as diplomats. Nicolson wrote many books of literary criticism and a biography of George V, was a Member of Parliament for ten years and was married to Vita Sackville-West and, despite both being incorrigibly homosexual, they produced two distinguished sons: Nigel, himself an author and the co-founder of Weidenfeld and Nicolson, and the art historian, Benedict.

Nigel published the letters and diaries of his father; I think it was Auberon Waugh who said at the time Nigel was more concerned with advancing his cause with his bank manager than advancing his father's reputation. *Journey to Java* scarcely gets a mention and it is undeniably the least known of his works, but nonetheless I rank it as a classic travelogue. What's more it is wholly original in its effortless investigation into the nature of melancholy.

Index

A. & C. Black 62

Africa xiii, 6, 42–44, 72, 111 *see also* Central African Republic, Kenya, South Africa, Zimbabwe

Ailesbury, Marquess of 80

Alanbrooke, Field Marshal 43

Alatas, Mishal 30

Amoco 101

Anglo-Hong Kong Trust 77

Anglo-Irish Corporation 32

Anguilla 4, 5

Anker-Simmons, Starr 49–50, 51

Annabel's 7, 40

Army 9, 17–23, 50, 84, 99 *see also* Caledonians, Grenadier Guards, Guards Independent Parachute Company, Gurkhas, Irish Guards, Royal Horse Guards, SAS

Asquith, Lady 28

Auchinleck, Field Marshal 43

d'Avigdor-Goldsmid family 11

Bamberg, Harold 23

Baring, Maurice 114–115, 139–40

Baring, Peter 104

Barings Bank 102, 103–104

Barrow, Julian 88, 91

Algy Cluff

By the Way...

FOREWORD BY
Charles Moore

From the Foreword by Charles Moore

'Algy is a great reader, and has a lovely, economical literary style, but he writes chiefly about characters unknown to the world of letters. They emerge fresh from these pages…

In his writing, he is himself a great memorialist of unusual customs, places and people – sharp, yet kind; sad, yet funny; modest, unique.'

Algy Cluff

Unsung Heroes

... and a few villains

FOREWORD BY
Simon Heffer

From the Foreword by Simon Heffer

'What flows from these pages are not just good stories about fine people, but a strong sense of what the author has in common with them – a sense of humanity and service. He also laments the passing of types that adorned our lives but, in a very different age, hardly now do so at all.'

Algy Cluff

Get On With It

A Memoir

FOREWORD BY
A. N. Wilson

From the Foreword by A. N. Wilson

There's nothing worth the wear of winning,
But laughter and the love of friends

'Algy's life bears this out. This book is the opposite of a misery memoir. It rejoices in his kind parents, his good friends and his happy marriage with three splendid sons. His boldness in the field of business and his merriment as a companion have their reward.'